SMILE

Into Your Precious Life

With the Marvels of

Mindfulness

A Guide to the Friends,

Teachers,

and Guardians that Support Us

on the Path of Goodness, Discovery,

and Truth

Mark W. Gebert

Copyright

© Copyright 2023 Mark W Gebert

All rights reserved.

This book is protected by the copyright laws of the United States of America. No part of this publication may be reproduced, stored in a retrieval system, or transmitted in any form or by any means without the prior permission of the copyright owner.

Ebook: 978-1-959901-27-3
Paperback : 978-1-959901-28-0
HardCover: 978-1-959901-29-7

A simple Smile aligns the heart
and mind effortlessly and naturally
brings joy and acceptance.
You also incline toward friendliness
with affection in your speech
and action.
Smile into your precious human life.
This is a good news story of the Marvels of
Mindfulness.

Acknowledgements

Although I was truly blessed to come to mindfulness and the teachings early in my adult life, it took a lifetime to fully appreciate the enormity of the question asked of me by my teacher Joseph Goldstein in 1974: "Can you simply be aware?" This sparked the beginning of a deep understanding that with mindfulness and its friends, which I call the Marvels of Mindfulness, there can be a transformation of all of your life.

I will always be profoundly grateful to Joseph, who was instrumental in my beginning the Path, as well as for his guidance and friendship all along the way. Also, to J. Krishnamurti, who brought investigation and a wisdom-based, "see for yourself" quality to my practice, along with spiritual courage and persistence. I give a deep bow to my lifelong spiritual friend Rodney Smith for his inspiration, wisdom, and encouragement these many years. Also, to my friend and guiding light, Narayan Liebenson, who has been, for more than 25 years, a reminder of the incredible warmth and purity of heart necessary to walk this lifetime journey with true gratitude and a smile. It is with great appreciation that I thank Lisa Story, my teaching partner and dear friend, for many wonderful years at metro Atlanta's Roswell Insight Meditation Community. My thanks also go to the RIMC community for their support, and the many teachers and friends who have influenced my journey. A heartfelt thank you to Joel Groover for being a wonderful spiritual friend, editor extraordinaire, as well as a "wise word wizard" for his many hours spent revising and improving my inspired labor of love.

To my parents, forever thanks for their protection, love, and guidance, which allowed me to prosper in an often-difficult life. To our children, Markus and Kimberly, may they continue to be a light of goodness in this world. Finally, to my wife Veletta, who has taught me the meaning of true love for over 40 years and continues to be a selfless example of purity and goodness in the world. I said many years ago, if you are lucky an angel may come into your life, and if you're really lucky she will agree to spend her life with you. How really, really lucky I've been all these years.

May the Truth guide, protect, and love you!

Forward

I have known Mark for almost 50 years. We first met at the beginning of the first three-month course at the Insight Meditation Society in Barre, Massachusetts, in 1976. Having meditated for only a couple of years at this point, I was impressed that Mark had attended the previous three-month course in Bucksport, Maine, the year before. Here is someone who returned to sit a second long retreat, and I wanted to find out the details of the adventure I was about to face. I interrogated him until I felt his confidence merge with my own and knew that I, too, could do this.

Mark has always had the ability to encourage Dharma urgency in himself and others. He and I bonded over a mutual love of J. Krishnamurti, whom we would quote to one another for inspiration. One of the messages that we both connected with deeply was the intolerance Krishnamurti had for second hand methods. He said the only way to discover the truth was through your own means and resources, without relying on outside sources of knowledge or holders of the truth. Mark uses his Buddhist training to make the same passionate plea. The Pali word, Ehipassiko, "come and see for yourself," is encouraged repeatedly. He uses this word to express this path of liberation as a solitary adventure, where each traveler must uncover, explore, and assimilate those same truths the Buddha expounded upon 25 centuries ago. It is not sufficient to take the words of the Buddha and simply pronounce them as true. The full realization and embodiment of those fundamental truths is essential. We change not from knowing the Buddha's message but from living it as truth.

A persistent theme of the book is never relinquish your spiritual or human sovereignty. Authenticity is a word most of us do not fully understand. We usually think we can discover who we are by living without restraints and following our desires, but Mark knows that following our desires only leads to a deeper level of internal conflict. He explains that freedom lies in our ability to accept and accommodate all situations, pleasant and unpleasant, and teaches the true path of authenticity requires a shift away from seeking pleasure toward self- intimacy and trust. We need a quiet and nonjudgmental base grounded in insight and wisdom to challenge our deeply entrenched mental patterns. Freedom is freedom from conditioning, not blindly following our thought patterns.

Mark is a contemplative and a meditator at heart. He has used and ingested Insight Meditation as his path forward. It is a path he knows thoroughly and one in which he is well equipped to expound upon. *SMILE Into Your Precious Life, With the Marvels of Mindfulness* is foremost a practice manual, but tucked within his teachings are biographical indications of what stirred him at a very young age to involve himself in such rigorous practice. He grew up in a stressful family situation. The family was affluent but unhappy, and Mark often felt isolated and alone. Early on Mark had a "persistent dissatisfaction with everything (he) touched." It is clear he could have become despairing and angry from such a dysfunctional upbringing, but he channeled his dissatisfaction into spiritual urgency. Mark's urgency is on every page of this book. He understood early on that the only way forward was to fully understand his reactions to the present moment. He developed an uncompromising determination to move his spiritual journey forward through the entire array of life experiences. He knew that wisdom came not in the avoidance of life but within its full participation and understanding.

Many readers will find Mark's use of acronyms like S.M.I.L.E. (smile, mindfulness, investigation, letting go, equanimity) useful to help train themselves to move toward the difficult rather than avoid or turn away from pain and dissatisfaction. It is within the difficult that Mark shows that the deepest transformations lie. He also suggests the unassuming phrase "Keep it simple" as a way to avoid overthinking any situation that arises, and uses the phrase to indicate that peace lies not in the complexity of thought but in the simple spontaneity of being human. Mark also skillfully adds several meditative exercises to emphasize his points and to allow the reader to settle more deeply into the topic at hand.

As Mark makes explicitly clear, being human is not the art of perfection. It may surprise some of the readers that perfection has everything to do with saintliness but nothing to do with spiritual transformation. Spiritually, we grow out of the idea of being anything at all, including perfect, and from the ashes of those polar opposites arises the wholeness of spirit. There never was or could be anything wrong with us except in the minds of ourselves or others, where all distortions take root. Outside of the mind, everything is just as it is, and that is perfection.

Though this path may be solitary in its inward focus, no one walks alone. Sangha is not only available but necessary. Side by side with each other we bathe in the basic goodness of life, nurturing one another in countless ways. No one is inaccessible or isolated from the inclusiveness of spirit, and everyone who practices mindfulness will always and forever be included within the gentle kindness of clear seeing. Awareness is equally available to all. Now relax, release the worry of accomplishment and open to the messages of this book. This book, if you allow it, lights a clear path forward towards that basic goodness of heart that is intrinsic to that awareness. Such is the message of Mark Gebert's book, *SMILE Into Your Precious Life, With the Marvels of Mindfulness*. May you have a gentle and clear read.

Rodney Smith

Seattle, Washington

June, 2023

Rodney Smith is the Founding Teacher of the Seattle Insight Meditation Society. He has written several excellent books, including most recently *Touching the Infinite – A New Perspective on the Buddha's Four Foundations of Mindfulness*.

Table of Contents

Part 1 1
My Beginnings – Discovering Some of the Dearest Friends, Teachers of Transformation, and Guardians of the Heart

Introduction To Part 1....................... 2
Dearest Friends of Mindfulness, Teachers of Transformation, and Guardians of the Heart

Chapter 1... 4
Living in an Unsettled World With Goodness, Discovery, and Truth - Overview of SMILE

Chapter 2... 9
SMILE – An Acronym for Living in an Unsettled World - *A Guided Meditation – Transforming Physical Discomfort*

Chapter 3... 13
My Beginning – Spiritual Urgency/Existential Angst

Chapter 4... 18
Moving from Hopelessness to Hope

Chapter 5... 24
Moving from Hope to a Bedrock of Clear Seeing

Chapter 6... 28
Moving from Clear Seeing to a Bedrock of Spiritual Confidence From a Faith that is Verified

Skillful Tireless Effort:................................ 30
Skillful Resolve and Perseverance:................ 31
Skillful Patience:.. 32

xi

Fearless Investigation:.................................. 32

Chapter 7... 36

Moving to Ehipassiko – Come and See for Yourself

Chapter 8... 40

Moving With Clear Seeing into A Change of Heart

Our Forgiveness Meditation Exercise.................. 46

Reflections for a Skillful, Forgiving Life.............. 49

Chapter 9... 51

Moving With Clear Seeing to Realignment Beyond The Cushion – Skillful Means

Daily Practice:.. 52

Stealing A Moment (Flexibility):...................... 55

Nature:.. 57

Dedicating Your Practice:............................... 59

Loving Kindness:.. 60

Spiritual Community (Sangha):....................... 61

My Wish for All Beings................................ 64

Part 2... 65

As Life Unfolds An In-depth Look at the Dearest Friends of Mindfulness

Introduction To Part 2............................... 66

As Life Unfolds with Marvels and the Dearest Friends of Mindfulness

Chapter 10... 68

The Dearest Friends of Mindfulness and Awakening – Relevance for Practice

Chapter 11... 74

Mindfulness With Investigation

Chapter 12... 77

Energy – Benefits and Dangers

Chapter 13.. 82

Wise Natural Focus and Concentration

Concentration Exercise, Inclusive and Exclusive............. 87

Mindfulness/Awareness of Awareness Exercise – Moving into Choiceless Awareness.. 89

Chapter 14..92

Joy and Tranquility - Gladdening The Mind/Heart

Gratitude or Joy Exercise............................ 96

Chapter 15.. 98

Equanimity With Patience

Meditation Exercise Mindfulness With Its Dearest Friends................ 103

Part 3....................................... 106

Additional Friends, Teachers of Transformation, and Guardians of the Heart that Arrive Along the Way

Introduction To Part 3........................107

Additional Friends, Teachers, and Guardians that Arrive Along the Way

Chapter 16...111

Wisdom and Compassion

Compassion Through Forgiveness Caring for Yourself And Others...... 115

Chapter 17.................................... 117

Generosity and Morality

A Story for Reflection......................... 123

Chapter 18...................................... 124

Moving Away from Division Into Unity – 'Us and Them' Has Got to End

Loving Kindness Meditation..........................131

Chapter 19..132

Antidotes and Skillful Means For The Common Hindrances

Greed or Attachment to View:........................133

Fear:...135

Sloth and Torpor:..................................137

Restlessness:......................................137

Doubt and Procrastination:.........................138

Anger:...139

Fear Exercise Using SMILE Into SMILES..............142

Chapter 20.......................................146

Is There Relevance of Locus of Control to Our Spiritual Path?

Locus of Control Meditation Exercise...............150

Chapter 21.......................................152

The Far and Near Enemies of the Brahma-viharas

The Far Enemies:...................................153

The Near Enemies:..................................155

Skillful Means and Antidotes for the Far Enemies:..157

Skillful Means and Antidotes for the Near Enemies:.159

Chapter 22.......................................161

Be Here Now – But How? Is Psychological Time Real or an Illusion?

How to Be Here Now?................................162

Can Any Object of Mind or Body be Experienced Outside of the Present Moment?.. **162**

The Past and Future – How are they Created?.......... **163**

Meditation Exercise (15 or 20 Minutes) For 'Be Here Now – But How? **166**

Chapter 23...**169**

Thought in Meditation Friend or Foe and Does it Have to Go? (Anatta and More)

Meditation Exercise The Thinking Game............... **173**

Chapter 24...**176**

The Inherent Truth of Inclusivity

A Heart Which Includes all Beings: Inclusivity Mindfulness and Natural Loving Kindness Exercise **180**

Chapter 25...**183**

Learning to Dance With the Difficult With Gratitude and Appreciation

Gratitude Exercise...**187**

Chapter 26...**189**

SMILE – An Acronym for Living in an Unsettled World With Goodness, Discovery, and Truth

A Guided Exercise – Transforming Anger

Moving From SMILE to SMILES

Loving Kindness Through Engaged Purity of Heart....**197**

Smile – the Special Sauce of Heart and Wisdom Practices

About The Author..**199**

Index...**201**

Guidance for using all exercises and reflections:

Keep it simple and smile.

If possible, have a consistent routine – same time and place for your daily practice.

Sit in a comfortable alert posture.

Relax – this is very important.

Breathe naturally – let the breath breathe.

Use soft, affectionate mindfulness – this will help to be kind to yourself and not judge so much.

Lastly, read the exercises slowly and carefully with curiosity and receptivity – this will foster a willingness for wisdom to arise and may allow you to see anew.

If you prefer **guided exercises**, feel free to go to my website at **marvelsofmindfulness.org**. I have recorded each exercise from the book as well as a few extras and they are freely given.

Part 1

My Beginnings –
Discovering Some of the Dearest
Friends,
Teachers of Transformation,
and Guardians of the Heart

Introduction To Part 1

Dearest Friends of Mindfulness, Teachers of Transformation, and Guardians of the Heart

Each morning I wake up with a smile from gratitude and appreciation for this precious human life, with all its friends, teachers, and guardians, always dedicated to the happiness and freedom of all living creatures.

In the world of mindfulness (*sati*) and on the path of goodness, discovery, and truth, it is clear that you don't need to know all that is in the books in any spiritual library. Rather, only a handful of pages of essential universal teachings that are directly seen and understood experientially are needed to walk the path. In this book, I'll go through these essential simple (but not easy to do) teachings, friends, guides, and protectors, which I call dearest friends of mindfulness, teachers of transformation, and guardians of the heart, in the order they mostly arose for me naturally throughout my lifetime. All are guides and protectors of our natural goodness of heart necessary to remain true to the skillful direction of awakened values and just perhaps awakening. These are also the marvels of mindfulness, as they work to transform all the deep roots of greed, aversion, and delusion/confusion into a life of goodness, discovery, and truth.

This is the ultimate good news story, even with the many human difficulties and adversities along the way. Let's be grateful for the difficulties in life, as they can become friends, teachers, and guardians that open your eyes to the wonders and beauty of life that you weren't paying attention to before. Smile into your precious life and its marvels.

"If a child smiles, if an adult smiles, that is very important. If in our daily lives we can smile, if we can be peaceful and happy, not only we, but everyone, will profit from it. If we really know how to live, what better way to start the day than with a smile? Our smile affirms our awareness and determination to live in peace and joy. The source of a true smile is an awakened mind."

– Thich Nhat Hanh

Chapter 1

Living in an Unsettled World With Goodness, Discovery, and Truth - Overview of SMILE

Know you are loved and appreciated.

Our dearest friends of mindfulness, teachers of transformation, and guardians of the heart are all those events, people, teachings, factors of mind, and other things in life that have guided, molded, protected, nourished, and moved you forward on the ultimate path of awakening, even if you didn't understand, know it or like it at the time. Please don't overthink it because, at some point, all of life acts as a teacher and guardian if the mind is awake or aware with right view or wise perspective. These friends, teachers, and guardians are also protectors of our often hidden and forgotten birthright of natural goodness and affection of heart, which, when uncovered by clear seeing and wisdom, will accompany and support us throughout our precious journey.

Perhaps the first marvel to arise from mindfulness or awareness is the wisdom born of clear seeing. It is the key to the wise perspective that all of life becomes a classroom with the friends, teachers, and protectors you need. Smile—this is the most important story of your precious human life.

Friends, teachers, and guardians appear according to the unique conditioning and life circumstances of our individual journeys. Some of you will find deep wisdom very early on the path; for others, it may be self-forgiveness. Some will find compassion early on, and for others, this may be elusive.

Motivations to enter the path of goodness also vary – from deep urgency with angst from suffering (called samvega in Pali, the language of the early Buddhist teachings) to a drive for self-improvement or simple curiosity.

If you continue this lifelong journey, you will find each friend, teacher, and guardian in your own way and your own time. Be assured with deep faith and confidence (saddha) they will appear!

Over the years, I have worked with a number of easy-to-remember acronyms and phrases (for example, "keep it simple") as skillful means. These tools can be a very valuable aid to your insight practice along the way. They are particularly helpful when difficulty or doubt knocks on your door of life. I hope you will learn and find our new skillful meditation acronym, SMILE, useful.

This acronym, SMILE, is one I've developed and used during the past several years while helping to turn adversity into opportunity with our local sangha (spiritual friends). It has been used often by our meditation community, where I've been privileged to teach for many years. I hope this acronym will resonate with each of you and become a reliable friend and helper during these unsettled times.

This SMILE overview will be followed up by a much more in-depth view in Chapter 2, using our new acronym as a guided meditation when dealing with physical pain. Pain can result in some of our most common negative conditioned reactions. The world is built around avoiding all types of pain, whether physical or psychological.

Our acronym SMILE contains several of the most important friends, teachers of transformation, and guardians of the heart on the path, and it may be part of our "bag of skillful tools" as a remedy for many of our most common difficulties in life.

The first thing I added to our acronym SMILE, which I've found to be extremely helpful, is an actual physical smile, to begin with. I've used this for years, particularly when turning the difficult into darlings.

Let's begin. The S in SMILE contains the special sauce or first skillful action, with awareness, for all the insight and heart practices we use, which is our simple, what I call our Mona Lisa Smile. This small soft physical outer/inner smile brings a joy and affection to our awareness that says, "Welcome, you are accepted here," and brings other friends I'll mention in the pages to come.

The M in SMILE is for Mindfulness, which is perhaps our most important friend, teacher, and guardian and part of the bedrock of most all insight or discovery teachings. Without mindfulness, it is not possible to see clearly or to penetrate delusion and confusion.

Mindfulness leads to the I in SMILE, which is for Investigation, which is interest with a curiosity or probing quality to see the way things are. Investigation is crucial for wisdom to arise, but I'll say much more about this later.

Now we have Smile, Mindfulness, and Investigation. Investigation leads naturally to the L in SMILE, which is our first, simplest, and perhaps our most profound teaching of Letting go or, more deeply, Letting be. Deep letting be contains allowing or acceptance of what is in this moment, but of course, not what you always want in this moment.

The L for Letting go or Letting be naturally leads to the E in SMILE: Equanimity with engagement. As the mind releases a little or a lot from any object of mind, equanimity naturally arises and creates a foundation of balance which, as it deepens, allows for skillful and wise engagement. Why? Because you are now safe, which is also the bedrock of a warm, welcoming, and inclusive sangha and necessary for skillful engagement in the world.

I sincerely wish I had come to all these teachers of transformation and guardians of the heart that make up this acronym in my early practice years. I believe they would have helped transform my life with more wisdom and perhaps with much less heartache and confusion. However, in reality, life brings you the most important teachers and guardians only when you're ready to hear their message. I hope you are ready and will carry these teachings on SMILE with a smile from this day forward. If they become yours, your life will, with diligence, sincerity, and deep faith, realign toward goodness!

I also feel deep compassion and appreciation for all of those that came before me and suffered to find the keys to our awakening. Also, to the young man named Mark, that struggled so greatly for my freedom today.

These dearest friends, teachers of transformation and guardians of the heart, and others I offer in this book, I hope, will guide, protect, and bring love to each of you as you walk this path of goodness, discovery, and truth with wisdom and compassion for all.

"So… starting now, smile more often – and you'll not only be happier yourself, but you might end up spreading that happiness to those around you! … Because of your smile, you make life more beautiful."

– Thich Nhat Hanh

Chapter 2

SMILE – An Acronym for Living in an Unsettled World - *A Guided Meditation – Transforming Physical Discomfort*

Smile and let the teachings of goodness begin.

Let's practice our acronym, SMILE, so it hopefully starts to become yours as time goes on, especially during difficult or trying times.

Get comfortable but stay with alert relaxation. We are going to do a guided practice meditation using physical pain, as well as use some helpful strategies to deal with discomfort since it will inevitably arrive during any life, no matter your age. Physical pain was the first object I used at the beginning of my insight meditation practice to help develop equanimity. If you sit long enough or just live enough, you will get sore, and pain sensation is an important tangible object to learn to find balance of mind (with future importance for old age, sickness, etc.). Research into chronic bodily pain suggests that physical pain is a combination of the actual physical body pain, plus perhaps a much larger contribution in the addition of psychological pain from the mind's reaction.

The Buddha talked about the two arrows. The first is what happens to you – pain in the knee, for example. The second is your reaction, aversion, tension, etc., which increases the total pain/suffering significantly. So, the first arrow happens (physical pain), but with the second arrow, there is a choice of reactions. If you understand this and find equanimity, then there is a good chance of balance and relaxed mindfulness, which will diminish the total pain/suffering. It is also just possible the second arrow is never fired!

During our guided meditation to help skillfully deal with physical pain (as well as used for fear, anger, or other difficulties if they arrive), we'll use SMILE. Remember, I developed this as a skillful means tool some time ago to help turn all adversity into an opportunity for spiritual growth.

We all know pain (the first arrow), how it feels, and what conditioned reactions (the second arrow) are usually elicited by that physical pain. It happens in all our lives, so we must learn to skillfully respond and not fire off more arrows!

Start by finding a small, manageable pain in the body to practice with. Remember, this is a practice exercise, so not anything more (be sensible).

Relax the body and notice the energy of pain in the body, the movement, the ebb, and flow of sensations that appear to be solid but never are. Recognize, accept, and feel pain in the body because it's present. Notice the feeling tone and tightness or constriction, but don't add dialogue if possible. Remember, the body is always present (like the breath) and always in the present. It can also be the base camp, touchstone, and ground in meditation, so use it often and relax (super important).

Notice how pain feels in the body – it manifests in the body and colors the mind. The body is not the primary verbal storyteller; it's just that the mind's content seduces through thoughts, reactions (mind and body), etc. Don't buy the story, or it will follow you wherever you go and take you where it wants you to go. Smile – it's OK! The storyteller, which may feed pain, also doesn't have to be a problem. Just let it be since it's there, and turn down the volume of the dialogue by giving most of your attention to the actual sensation of body pain. Let's move to SMILE. Pause during the exercise where and when, as you see fit.

S   Now comes the S in SMILE, which is to have an actual soft physical outer/inner smile (our Mona Lisa smile). Our Smile is our first skillful action and will help the early surrender into this moment with pain. This is a surrender from strength, not weakness, with an attitude of acceptance that says, "You can't hurt me anymore"! This also does not mean giving in and giving it to another. In the first instant of this soft smile – feel the sea/see change that reduces the anxious or unacceptable aspects of pain because it says welcome, come in, my friend pain, you are accepted and appreciated as my teacher.

M   This smile and attitude change allows you to naturally come to the M in SMILE, which is our accepting affectionate Mindfulness. Allow mindfulness to arise as early as you can before any other reactions or unhelpful commentary are given. Smile – wisdom will begin to teach you now because mindfulness will bring...

I   one of its first dearest friends, Investigation, which is a wisdom factor of clear seeing and the I of SMILE. Investigation will work to see how pain can easily bring aversion and lots of arrows if we buy the quiver of arrows it offers. Physical pain will come in all lives and is designed biologically as an important protector, but if not dealt with wisely can certainly impede a skillful life. Smile; you can make friends with whatever knocks at your door of life. Investigation will bring you to the question, "Can I (the mind) relax and accept even this difficulty with balance?" With the arrival of wisdom from investigation, our first and one of the most important teachings also arrives, and we come to the L in SMILE, which is …

L   Letting go – No push, no pull. Just let go or, deeper, let be (one of our most basic and profound teachers all along the way). With letting go, the energy of pain or suffering will continue to change and perhaps lose its grip on you (mind/body). If it is not refueled by dialogue and reactive energies, we perhaps see a deeper letting be where pain continues to lose its power and more clearly becomes a friend, teacher, and guardian.

E   You may have already noticed, beginning with letting go (and becoming more complete with letting be), that the E in SMILE has arrived. This is Equanimity, the natural ground of the mind/body process. Equanimity is one of the most stable and balanced friends of mindfulness and virtually all meditation practices. It will become a trusted and reliable companion as you practice and move toward freedom from pain in your precious human life. Smile as our marvels continue.

Chapter 3

My Beginning – Spiritual Urgency/Existential Angst

I'm happy you are here.

As a reminder, you don't need to know all of what's in the books in a spiritual library, but rather only a handful of pages of essential, universal teachings found in what I call the dearest friends, teachers of transformation, and guardians of the heart. In this book, I'll go through these friends, teachers, and guardians in mostly the order they arose naturally for me as I walked and continue to walk on the path of goodness, discovery, and truth (awakening).

Some of this will be my personal story and perhaps painful for some of you as you hear your own story in mine. No worries, we will walk together in safety as sangha or spiritual friends.

As a reminder, the order that each friend, teacher, and guardian appeared to me may, and most likely will, differ from yours, as we each bring our conditioning and life circumstances to our unique individual journeys.

As you sit quietly with your practice of mindfulness during insight meditation (or any other practice of goodness and discovery) you will meet some of the earliest friends, teachers, and guardians, which are Universal truths of all conditioned life, whether we like it or not. They include the fact that constant change (anicca) is our only constant. If all things change to their core, then even our belief in a permanent self is in question (the teaching of anatta points to the unreality of any permanent self or essence). If we cling to anything that changes, we may get rope burn, suffer, or have unreliability and unsatisfactoriness (dukkha) as nothing, if examined closely, remains the same. Of course, see for yourself.

I come from the school of what I call "keep it simple," so my simple meaning of friends, teachers, and guardians is all those events, people, teachings, factors of mind, and other things in life that have guided, molded, protected, nourished, and moved you forward on the path of awakening, even if you didn't understand, know it or like it at the time. Don't overthink it because, at some point, all of life's moments act as a teacher if the mind is awake or aware with the wise perspective of seeing things as they truly are.

If you continue this lifelong journey, you will find each friend, teacher, and guardian in your own way and your own time, and as I said, be assured with deep faith and confidence they will appear!

Many of us overthink things and believe that the more we know and carry, the better off we will be! This may be true for your job and other parts of life, but on the spiritual journey, those who travel lightest often progress the fastest and farthest.

Life is hard – our backpack is so crammed with our beliefs and problems from the past, and fears of the future that we get bogged down. If our backpack is too heavy, we tire out, slow down, and may eventually give up, saying, "I can't do it." This is delusional doubt, as opposed to healthy skepticism rooted in wisdom, and can be a major hindrance for spiritual progress.

We almost always start our spiritual journey with a full heavy backpack because we don't know mindfulness and the simple teachings of letting go or letting be and putting down what is no longer useful. My full heavy backpack was stuffed with affluence, dysfunction, and dissatisfaction when my practice began. What is in your backpack? Ask yourself.

I was raised by two alcoholic parents, and my mom had psychiatric issues. Very affluent, but little real joy. There was constant fighting, waking up in the middle of the night, and huddling in fear with my brother and sister. We heard my parents yell phrases like "living with the enemy" and "I hate you" (often followed by regrets and makeup sessions). I saw dysfunction at a level that was totally unacceptable for almost all the families I knew but was the norm for me and my siblings. Our family would much rather be right and fight than be happy!

We were caught by the trappings of "the good life" – cars, houses, and strong "I'm right" opinions. There often was very little real joy or happiness and major unsatisfactoriness as nothing was ever good enough. We had the means to buy more stuff to try to be "happy," but little changed or improved as I finished my teenage years. So where did all the dysfunction and family issues go? Yep, in my backpack! So, of course, my backpack of life contained lots of destructive and unskillful lessons, and I was becoming them.

One Friday night, I made a mistake I had never made: I got stuck at home by myself. I called everyone I knew out of desperation to avoid a loneliness I couldn't or wouldn't bear. Who do you think I got? Absolutely no one!

A deep, cold fear of loneliness and isolation seemed to be crawling out of the dark corners of my mind. All this and more had all gone into my backpack, which now was breaking me from the weight.

I had suffered from a "curse," or so I thought, from as early as I could remember – a persistent dissatisfaction with everything I touched. Even when I got exactly what I wanted – for example, to be the guy in the nice car, with a girlfriend, lots of drugs, etc. – it just wasn't good enough. No matter what, unsatisfactoriness would quickly return! Where did this unhappiness go? You know!

I was beginning to finally see and understand a tiny bit that all my existence contained an element of unsatisfactoriness or just plain suffering and that I was marinating in it. I knew I couldn't go forward. The backpack was just too heavy. It was crushing me! It all went into my backpack: the anger, loneliness, and fear, the feeling that I was letting my family down, the sense that I had no friends who truly understood me, as well as that clear understanding that I wasn't going to make it. A deep, pervasive sense of hopelessness arose in me. There was nowhere to turn and nowhere to run – no escape from this heavy and dark doubt, full of delusion and confusion.

What had knocked or more accurately, banged on my door of life was uninvited, unintended, and unappreciated (at least at the time). I learned much later there was a Buddhist term for what I was going through. Traditionally, samvega refers to either spiritual urgency or existential angst. Both had arrived simultaneously at my life's doorstep.

It all happened as I was finishing my junior year in college and realizing that I could find no meaning in my "chosen" major, business. Everything inside me was in flux. I was questioning everything I believed amid a sense of deep, pervasive fear and turmoil. I knew I couldn't and wouldn't be going into business as had been expected in my family for generations. I finished my degree but felt disillusioned, alienated and that my life was becoming meaningless. I had no interest in the "bright," successful future mapped-out for me, much to my entire family's dismay and disappointment.

Losing my "future" at 22 years old brought with it seemingly unanswerable questions: Why am I here? Does life have any meaning? Who or what am I? Can I find purpose in my life? Will I survive and fit in somewhere? No doubt you recognize some of these same questions. What's still weighing your backpack down?

Chapter 4

Moving From Hopelessness to Hope

It all started with a single book.

Seeing that I was miserable and had nowhere to turn, a friend of mine who had started to explore Eastern philosophy handed me a copy of Be Here Now by Ram Dass. As I leafed through the pages, to my surprise, a flicker of light went on, and a small but noticeable joy from hope appeared. Importantly, there was also a glimmer of something I'll discuss in more detail in a later chapter: doubt driven by wisdom. This was distinct from the huge amount of worrying about the future – a form of doubt guided by delusion and confusion – that I had felt before. Rather than shouting, this new doubt whispered silently to me, "There may be a different way to live your life and survive."

Being lost and unemployed (which did not thrill my parents), I accepted an invitation to drive some friends to take a six-week class with Ram Dass at the Naropa Institute (now Naropa University) in Boulder, Colorado. The Tibetan master Chögyam Trungpa had founded the learning center that same year (1974). I had already seen that, at least for me, accumulating more wealth and possessions would not bring lasting peace or happiness. To realize there were "alternative" lifestyles pursuing and emphasizing joy, happiness, and something called truth or awakening was a turning point.

At Naropa, you had Ram Dass, who had attracted hundreds of Western Hindu followers, all dressed in white flowing clothes, with long hair and beards, and clutching prayer beads. In contrast, you had hundreds of Trungpa's Buddhist followers in street clothes, along with his Vajra Guard (protectors) in formal suits! Remember, I'm just a kid from Philly still hoping someone would save me. Here you had a little clash of two religious cultures, which made me feel at home a bit with all the conflict (joke).

After I arrived at Naropa, my first meditation instruction was uneventful, as I had no clue what the instructor was talking about. I kept looking and saw a small sign posted on a message board about another person teaching something called "Insight meditation."

It was there I met this American teacher named Joseph Goldstein, who had just returned from eight years of intensive practice and study in India. He seemed so "regular" and spoke in clear, simple language which I could understand. He knew I suffered and smiled and said a phrase that caused a "sea/see change." He said at some point, "Can you simply be aware?" and that's all I remember. There came an epiphany and joy from hope, and a light went on. I began to know I had a purpose – that perhaps I could and would survive. I still didn't really know how to meditate or be aware, but I finally had at least some direction to move toward.

I left Naropa after six weeks with some bounce in my step and some hope in my heart and went hitchhiking for six weeks out West. I still had no real sense of how to meditate, but I had heard before I left Naropa that Joseph and his fellow Insight teachers Jack Kornfield (who I had also met) and someone named Sharon would maybe do some retreats in the future if there was any interest. I really didn't have a clue of what a retreat was or meant.

After about a year or more of continued loneliness, doubt, and uncertainty, I again knew something in my life had to change. I had been trying to meditate regularly with little instruction and no support. I was isolating from my friends, who were still drinking and taking drugs, etc., and I had started working construction, to my parents' disbelief and disappointment. The phone rang in the late summer of 1975, and Sharon Salzberg, whom I had never met, told me about an upcoming three-month retreat in Bucksport, Maine. She had learned about me from Joseph and was happy I would be attending the retreat, in part because the organizers planned to rent space in a Catholic monastery and needed commitments.

It was a strange time for me. My father and mother were now attempting to stay sober and, like me, find a path that would lead to a better life. My dad kissed me on the cheek when I left for my retreat, which was very sweet and had never happened up to that time. I gave my mom 23 (my age) roses as I left, knowing I would not be back until I found the deep change or the "something" I needed. She cried – which also sent me off with some sweetness in my heart.

Of course, I was going by myself to something called a three-month retreat and was scared. I was also excited by the prospect of meeting nice friends over what I thought would be a pitcher of beer and lobster and, of course, doing some meditation as well. It became very scary when I heard as the retreat was starting that there would be no talking (I guess no friends), all vegetarian (no lobster), and there would be something called precepts (so no drinking, sex, etc.). Also, no writing, reading, and no phone calls unless it was an emergency. All day every day, we would be sitting and doing something called "walking meditation," which I had not done. It was all quite a surprise, but I signed on and stayed. I knew I had nowhere else to go for relief in this whole world.

It was extremely hard for me as I realized I was one of the few beginners (most of them left after the first two weeks). I also felt that I was in way over my head – surrounded by ex-monks and long-term Western practitioners returning from practice in Thailand, India, and other South Asian Buddhist countries.

As you might expect, all my problems came with me and began to appear quickly. I was scared, desperately lonely, and way under-experienced in mindfulness practice, never having heard of equanimity, tranquility, or rapture. However, I did have energy, a yeoman's effort, and loads of overthinking – a challenging combination on a three-month meditation retreat!

After the first three weeks, I had what I learned later was a profound "dark night of the soul." The experience was not "of me" in the sense that it was not about my personal psychological and emotional material so much as the deep, terrifying realization that there was nowhere for me to go and no way for me to escape the unfolding that was happening. This included a "dissolution" experience, with no safety net left and nothing to hold on to. There had been a significant mental alignment shift, but the terror of no footing continued. I talked with the teachers and quickly realized that no one outside of me could really help me. I had to learn this lesson alone, a process that had started even before I arrived at the retreat.

I became extremely sick and went through what you could think of as an involuntary body cleansing, eating very little and lying in bed in my little cubicle for a whole week. As I continued to get sicker, I decided to leave for a few weeks to go home and get well. When I arrived home, my dad and mom were happy but shocked at my appearance. I had gone from 130 to 113 lbs. in four weeks.

I returned for the last six weeks of the retreat. I was physically healthy but still very worried about going back to the "terror" as I approached the monastery. To my amazement, no terror arrived, and everything was different, like magic or Grace. Some "gifts" had arrived from this experience of realignment that, once again, were "not of me." All of a sudden, I had some understanding of mindfulness and concentration. A sense of anatta, with fullness and equanimity, arose. Forgiveness and other gifts like self-kindness and patience that were also not of me arrived. Loneliness evaporated and, to this day, has never returned. Fear did not show its face again at that retreat, and I needed very little sleep, just two hours a night.

I left changed and charged, with greater resolve and self-reliance, and spiritual confidence or trust in the accuracy of the teachings. I also knew that mindfulness was, in fact, our great protector, and I began to see some other of the dearest friends, teachers of transformation, and guardians of the heart. I had a clear, certain direction in my life. The "Dharma hook" was deeply embedded in my heart. My hopelessness had finally moved to a foundation of renewed hope. The marvels of mindfulness were finally released to help transform this once lonely, chronically unsatisfied, and directionless young man. A truly marvelous story of transformation and goodness!

"By watching yourself in your daily life with alert interest, with the intention to understand rather than to judge, in full acceptance of whatever may emerge because it is there, you encourage the deep to come to the surface and enrich your life and consciousness with its captive energies. This is the great work of awareness. It removes obstacles and releases energies by understanding the nature of life and mind. Intelligence is the door to freedom, and alert attention is the mother of intelligence."

– Sri Nisargadatta

Chapter 5

Moving From Hope to a Bedrock of Clear Seeing

I wish you hope!

In the darkness, my first teacher Joseph Goldstein showed me the possibility of a light I didn't know existed – the light of mindfulness. A light he learned from his teacher, who learned from his teacher all the way back 2,500 years to Siddhartha Gautama, the Buddha. As this light began to shine within me, all aspects of my life gradually began to transform. Since then, I've seen again and again that mindfulness is our most important friend, teacher, and guardian of the heart. Without its presence, we cannot see clearly or penetrate delusion and confusion, which is necessary for wisdom and other marvels to arise.

So, what is mindfulness/awareness? Insight teacher Sylvia Boorstein offers the most accurate definition I've heard: "Mindfulness is the aware, balanced acceptance of the present experience. It isn't more complicated than that. It is opening to or receiving the present moment, pleasant or unpleasant, just as it is, without either clinging to it or rejecting it."

Mindfulness naturally brings investigation, which will help bring wisdom. Investigation sees the interplay of mind objects and bodily reactions – for example, how anger, if not skillfully dealt with, can burn you first and poison and harden your heart with hatred. Investigation is the inquisitive, pattern-seeking part of mindfulness and also the part that brings interest. This is super important, because it leads to more energy and focus, a natural unification of mind.

These factors help us overcome difficult lessons and transform them into vehicles for growth.

Pema Chödrön says, "It isn't the things that happen to us in our lives that cause us to suffer, it's how we relate to the things that happen to us that cause us to suffer. If we learn to open our hearts, anyone, including the people who drive us crazy, can be our teacher." Can we see this? Yes, of course, we can and will as we continue to walk the path together.

How does hope transform into a bedrock of clear seeing from mindfulness? In each moment of mindfulness with investigation, there is a retraining and addition of wholesome mind factors. A mini-transformation is taking place in each moment of mindfulness. A realignment of the mind always in the direction of what I call awakened values (honesty, integrity, kindness, inclusiveness, etc.), discovery, insight, and perhaps awakening!

Why? Because mindfulness brings its dearest friends or wholesome mind factors to the "party" and balances several mind factors which are crucial for insight and, ultimately, awakening. These factors are investigation, energy, joy or rapture, tranquility or relaxation, focus (concentration), and importantly – equanimity or balance of mind.

Mindfulness, with its awakening friends, constantly works in concert to begin to allow wisdom to be found in not only each of the difficulties of your life, perhaps the richest soil for wisdom to grow, but all of your life to guide you.

You begin to see choices you didn't know you had. For example, stepping out of the way if a poison arrow is fired or adversity comes your way. Also, if the heart is open with equanimity, there may be no target for the poison arrow to hit and no or very few buttons to push. Which means many fewer triggers and a true sense of safety, considered the bedrock of spiritual friendship.

Can we learn to respond with wisdom and not constantly react from decades old unwise conditioning? Here's the way out. It's easy to say, but of course, difficult at times to do.

Important: Mindfulness provides a small space or momentary silent reflection for what is called the "sacred pause" that, with presence, allows all of us to respond skillfully instead of just react. There is a huge difference in our life when we are mindful and can access this sacred pause and respond out of wisdom instead of reactive conditioning.

Many emotions are deeply conditioned with reactive mind states, so we need to bring awareness to respond safely to ourselves and others as early as possible. This can be difficult, so be kind to yourself. It is a lifelong work in progress but will eventually allow you to be a "refuge" of safety for others and for the world community.

In each moment of mindfulness with investigation and interest, there is a realignment and development of these dearest friends, teachers, and guardians as wholesome factors of mind. As this alignment happens gradually or quickly in your life, all aspects eventually move in the direction of wisdom, loving kindness or affection, compassion, forgiveness, patience, gratitude, inclusivity, and other goodness factors. The good news is this alignment and transformation, from hope to trust and confidence, unfolds naturally as you continue mindfully with your interest to see and know, walking with diligence and sincerity throughout all facets of what is becoming a skillful life of goodness.

Mindfulness with investigation also brings a natural morality: Greater generosity, harmony in livelihood, skillful speech, honesty, and affection for all.

It is these friends, teachers, and guardians that start to help transform hope into a bedrock of faith or confidence in the truth – grown from wisdom and compassion, all born from clear seeing as the path of goodness and discovery becomes illuminated.

Chapter 6

Moving From Clear Seeing to a Bedrock of Spiritual Confidence From a Faith that is Verified

I wish you faith and courage!

Walking the path of discovery and truth requires a verified faith (never blind). This spiritual confidence/courage allows us to walk through the many dark valleys in a human life. It is especially important for all of us who choose with open eyes and an open heart to face and turn toward our adversities knowing they are friends, teachers, and guardians and the richest soil of all for spiritual growth!

In this chapter, I'm going to discuss in some detail the importance of a spiritual confidence or courage that ultimately must be verified by a bedrock of clear seeing. Spiritual confidence is a blend of mental factors which results in the ability to stay the course on the path even when friends, family, fear, and conditioning say otherwise. It's about having the courage to welcome your fears and the "unwanted" as friends and teachers and to always remember that you walk this path for all sentient beings, which strengthens your resolve.

In my darkest hours of walking the path, after I knew I had nowhere to go and no one could "save" me, the clear seeing from mindfulness with wisdom arose. It brought with it not only a sense of ehipassiko or come and see for yourself, but also, in tandem, a spiritual confidence which I never lost but is at times challenged by life even today.

This spiritual confidence is driven even today by faith and courage that – here's the important part – is verified by the clear seeing of mindfulness and confirmed by wisdom and compassion. You have a deep sense that you can do this because you can do this! It's the confidence, never blinded by mere opinion, that comes from seeing, not from thinking (important).

Here is another beauty of a faith or confidence that is verified – it becomes a sense of taking things as they truly are or come-what-may appreciation for the teacher of the moment and a life's full range of friends, teachers, and guardians. Verified faith allows you to answer whatever knocks on your door with a smile. You can even offer a welcome of some, metaphorically speaking, "tea and goodies" – and actually mean it.

To welcome with acceptance just what it is, as it is, allows you (the mind) to not give it a past or imprint it. And because of that, it will not have a grip on your future, either. To trust mindfulness and its friends to walk this journey with you is one of the jewels or keys to transformation.

Spiritual confidence also brings another gift: a verified faith in the goodness and teaching/transformation potential of life. You develop a deep trust that it is unfolding in the direction of what I will call awakened values like generosity, kindness, patience, gratitude, and others, with a smile and appreciation.

The blend of mental factors (or perhaps attitudes of mind) that largely make up spiritual confidence includes skillful tireless effort, unwavering resolve and perseverance, gentle, skillful patience, and fearless investigation. The foundation for all these, of course, is the clear seeing of mindfulness with its dearest friends.

Skillful Tireless Effort: (particularly with the difficult)

This mental factor is about relaxed and continuous effort to be mindful of whatever is present in each moment, including even subtle forms of greed and aversion. A simple formula: What you want to hold on to is greed; what you want to get rid of is aversion. Think of greed and aversion as being two sides of the same coin. Mindfulness is the rim, the third side. It provides balance.

Be guided by skillful, balanced effort – calm, grounded, affectionate, and soft, never regarding what you find as too much or too little, and always motivated by dedication to the real happiness and freedom of all sentient beings.

"It's an effort that might be unrecognizable to those who think 'effort' means trying hard. You have to try soft – to be curious and open to whatever it is that results. Effort doesn't mean gritting your teeth and pushing through to the other side: it means sitting where you're stuck and not running away."

– Nancy Thompson

Skillful Resolve and Perseverance:

Contains a faith or confidence full of wisdom that the teaching is true, that the truth is already within you and can be realized by you, right where you are sitting. Be confident you can do this!

This resolve and perseverance must be unwavering because, from a Buddhist perspective, if you believe someone or something outside of yourself can "save you," you may or will leave the path. Remember what ails you – your fears, anger, and difficulties – will follow you no matter where you go. You will eventually know that the difficult, when faced, can teach, protect, and allow spiritual growth in very fertile soil.

This resolve and perseverance are part of not running away, based on a wisdom and resolve that is stronger than the fear of the difficult or doubt, which is part of spiritual confidence. In my opinion, this doesn't mean you have to engage in what could be unskillful perseverance (three-hour mandatory sittings, no sleeping laying down, sitting cross legged if you can't, etc.). We're not here to "break or annihilate the self" but to see clearly and transform, through wisdom and compassion, our heart and mind.

Spiritual confidence or faith allows you to stick to the point and persevere to the end. It's a simple resolve to stay the course. What choice do you have? Run, and you are chased. Avoid the difficult, and whatever you are running from will come back stronger and will visit again for sure.

Faith or confidence with wisdom gives you certainty that this, too, will change. You gain a willingness to see any mental state or emotion, including fear or anger, to its end. This is the good news part of change/impermanence, that even the difficulties change and pass away.

Skillful Patience:

Calmness, acceptance, and allowing of what is in this moment with equanimity or balance is one of the gifts of mindfulness. You see that even the difficult is warmed and transformed by wisdom, affection, and patience. Remember to always smile into adversity if you can.

Spiritual patience is similar to conventional patience but requires a very long view and a gentle perseverance to continue your practice no matter what. When you "hit a rough patch" full of hindrances, to carry on knowing you have a dedicated practice larger than yourself. Remember that difficulties in practice can be either demons or darlings depending on our reaction (acceptance versus judgments, etc.)

Fearless Investigation:

And lastly, we have deep, fearless investigation as part of spiritual confidence or verified faith.

Fearless investigation sees the movement and intention silently of mind objects and the many reactions in the body, especially with, for example, fear. Fear can put you in a dark corner of the mind and can poison, harden, and color your heart. If fear is not skillfully dealt with, you can come to fear the whole world and everyone in it.

Remember to keep it simple. Mindfulness naturally brings its friend deep, fearless investigation. The two often move in tandem, giving rise to a wise perspective and a larger view grounded in clear seeing. For example, by refusing to capitulate to doubt and fear on the path, by seeing that these too will pass, you gain even more confidence in the larger perspective of, "It's OK; you can do this." By contrast, running away generally feeds the difficult and allows it to grow. See for yourself.

> *"Every day, think as you wake up, today, I am fortunate to be alive, I have a precious human life; I am not going to waste it. I am going to use all my energies to develop myself, to expand my heart out to others, to achieve enlightenment for the benefit of all beings. I am going to have kind thoughts towards others; I am not going to get angry or think badly about others. I am going to benefit others as much as I can."*
>
> – The Dalai Lama

Finally, for me, it was wisdom with compassion that helped me realize that my practice was always for the happiness and freedom of all beings, not just me. It was a practice much larger than myself – a dedicated practice I did for all beings that led to this deeper fearless investigation and confidence, which Pema Chödrön calls "outrageous courage." It becomes the confidence to walk this path no matter what for the happiness and freedom of all beings, a Bodhisattva.

But at times, there will be things you don't want to see or perhaps aren't ready to see. Don't look for trouble, as my teacher Joseph would say. Know your limits, but they must be guided by wisdom and compassion, not fear! Remember, this confidence or faith is not a blind faith, but rather, one that is always verified by the clear seeing of mindfulness and truth.

Lastly, always walk the path at your pace, but you must take the walk – no one can do it for you. Never believe you can't do it, and also remember, in each moment of mindfulness there is, in fact, a mini-transformation taking place, always in the direction of purity, affection of heart, and goodness. A true marvel.

Chapter 7

Moving to Ehipassiko – Come and See for Yourself

I wish you clear seeing!

As described in Chapter 3, I had a deep, difficult, but transforming early experience at 23, which never allowed me to leave the path. Although this experience was initially extremely difficult, many friends, teachers, and guardians began to arrive in time with gifts, including an unshakeable understanding of the accuracy of the teachings, of unwavering resolve, of anatta, affection, forgiveness, suffering, and much more. For me, I knew I had nowhere else to go and lost the ability to leave the path from that point forward. But it was hard, stepping away from friends and family, lack of support, little access to sangha or community support, and often by myself. My doubts had turned from delusion and confusion to a different sense of doubt, as part of a questioning that is guided by wisdom from clear seeing, but it was also still a difficult period in my life.

Remember, in my darkest hour, after I knew no one from outside could "save" me, the clear seeing from mindfulness with wisdom eventually gave rise to a spiritual confidence (I talked about this in our last chapter), but not until I began to understand one of the simplest and most important teachings required to continue walking any path of goodness and truth.

That teaching or teacher is ehipassiko (come and see for yourself). It is the heart of the wisdom of direct experiential seeing of the ever-present now. The Buddha said, "Don't believe me but see for yourself if the teaching is true by your own direct knowing of this moment just as it is." Not as you think it is, as I've said for many years.

Ehipassiko was one of the big attractions for me on this path, as the teaching was not meant to be adopted from blind faith, which never worked for me, but rather from a confidence from direct seeing that arose from investigation with wisdom. Not from mere thinking or because someone else (even a teacher) said it was true. Almost all major religions have an element of blind following or blind faith, sometimes with very dangerous results.

Some of the ingredients that go into ehipassiko include a relaxed earnest effort to inquire, curiosity, and a wisdom based on skeptical doubt (I was born with this). These all arise with mindfulness to investigate and a clarity to see for yourself this ever-present now. With the wisdom factors of investigation, curiosity, and inquiry, an interest with natural focus will arise to learn from the teaching or truth of this moment that is always present and available.

But you must do the work yourself to see if what is said is true. A teacher, no matter how experienced or wise, can only point the way. You must walk the path yourself, as no one can step in for you, although teachers, sangha, and others can and do certainly provide much needed support throughout your journey.

Even the Buddha, upon his enlightenment, was not sure if he would teach or how he would teach as he realized no external force or doctrine, no rituals, could free you. But he knew he could provide accurate teaching and skillful means as a guide, as a path map. His essential teachings, which he once likened to "a handful of leaves" versus an entire forest of knowledge, are extremely accurate. But of course, always come back to see for yourself if these profound teachings are true. I realized early on that direct seeing clearly, not blind belief, was the necessary factor for wisdom and insight of any kind to arise.

This teaching is simple (not easy), practical, and always a direct application of the Middle Way with no extremes. It is simply the wisdom of seeing for yourself the ever present now. No secret teachings or magical or fanciful thinking involved. The essence of teaching is the same for monks and laypeople, so all can and do walk this path equally. There is no "hopeium" in the teaching, but rather a good news story of liberation and the real possibility of living a kind, wise, skillful life.

Ehipassiko asks who and what do you trust? Ultimately this comes from listening to your compassionate wisdom with investigation. Know you have the seeds of truth and freedom already; our practice just waters and fertilizes them. This essence of the truth is in all of us, but it flowers on its own, not based on when or how you want it to.

Finally, remember ehipassiko wears the fragrance of skillful skeptical doubt with wisdom and deep interest to come see for yourself. It can bring some angst or uneasiness initially in a meditation practice as difficulty or uncertainty may be seen on the path. However, consistent daily practice will help all the teachings, including ehipassiko, grow naturally in your life and often pull the plug on many difficulties before they fully bloom. Smile.

"Believe nothing merely because you have been told it, or because it is traditional, or because you yourself have imagined it. Do not believe what your teacher tells you merely out of respect for the teacher. But if by thorough examination you find a path leading to good and happiness for all creatures, follow it like the moon in the path of stars."

– The Buddha (adapted by Sujata)

Chapter 8

Moving With Clear Seeing Into a Change of Heart

Know you can do this.

In this chapter, I'll speak about one of the most important friends, teachers, and guardians and an integral part of the essentials for a skillful life. As I've said for many years, through mindfulness and reflection, we know better than to burn bridges, battle others over opinions and spread anger/animus toward anyone, even your supposed enemy.

We know better – although, as ordinary people who suffer, we have an extraordinary opportunity, by seeing things clearly, to transform the heart and mind and live differently with affection. We have a right to suffer, but we also have a birthright to follow the path to freedom from suffering as well. We have a choice! We have to make the right, skillful choice and bring the light of mindfulness to the darkness in our life.

The goal is not to hold ourselves to an impossible standard of perfection; it's to see life as a work in progress. We will always have the opportunity to try again, to find forgiveness, and to know compassion for ourselves and, ultimately, everyone we meet.

This requires reflection and honesty about the things in our heart that keep us apart. It's not to judge ourselves but to see the truth with clarity.

Forgiveness with wisdom and compassion is one of the most important gifts on the path and hopefully in all human lives. It allows a true change of heart, fertilizes affection, and is also fertilized by affection. It guides you. As you show up each day and allow mindfulness to shine its bright light in all parts of your precious life, you get both gifts – forgiveness and affection – for free.

I want to be perfectly clear; forgiveness doesn't mean forgetting, dishonoring, or bypassing the past. It is important to learn when there is still productive soil in which to grow. Doing this work helps us recognize that none of us is perfect and that, generally, people were just doing the best that they could at that time. This helps us see through notions of "us" and "them." It can be the gateway to a true change of heart – a forgiveness so deep and purifying that you are no longer driven by the hurts of your past. This comes partly from the recognition that carrying the burdens of the past is a weight too heavy to carry forward in life. Wisdom with compassion present the very real possibility of putting down what is no longer skillful, useful, or wise to carry any longer.

Forgiveness was then and still is responsible for the biggest emptying of my backpack and traveling light in this lifetime! Forgiveness doesn't say the hurt never happened, but rather allows you to heal, learn and walk forward as your life is no longer controlled by the difficulties of a past you can't change.

Let's talk about the many transformative virtues of forgiveness and how it will allow you to arrive at "redemption, reconciliation and friendship" by remembering "forgiveness is not an occasional act, but it is rather a constant attitude," as Dr. Martin Luther King Jr. said in his 6 Principles of Nonviolence. It is an attitude that includes joy and affection and allows us to put down many of the harshest, most self-critical, and most self-centered aspects of our past.

Forgiveness comes from a deep realization that I'm not perfect, you're not perfect, and in reality, no one will be "Perfect" with a capital "P." Perfectionism is an exercise in suffering because everything is in constant change, including our definition of "Perfect." True perfection is always with a lowercase "p." It's about realizing the perfection of your and everyone else's imperfection. This means deep acceptance of what is and letting go of your image of what or how you think it should be. This transformation is always guided by the many teachers, protectors, and guardians that arrive in our lives. This includes realizing the perfection and completeness of the present moment, which is the only moment you have. The past is gone, and the future never arrives.

I've said many times in my life, "Forgive all before you walk out of the room." This includes yourself, but if you're wrong or hurtful, then asking for forgiveness immediately from all involved allows you to walk with more lightness and freedom.

This was an important part of the success for my dad's eventual recovery (41 years of sobriety) and 12 Step programs as well.

As you recall, I began my change of heart at 23 years old. I was broken from the weight of my past and the family burdens I carried from a dysfunctional family and my major dysfunctional responses. This came to a peak on my first long silent retreat when the weight of my past became a burden I could no longer carry. When the weight is too great to bear, Grace and inner freedom may not be far away if the heart is ready to transform.

My change of heart began in earnest with a few tears and a simple question which was: Did those who loved me the most, i.e., my family, with their eyes wide open and clear, also want to hurt me the most? I finally arrived at a resounding answer: No. For the first time, I realized that my parents did the "best they could or were able." They weren't perfect, and neither was I. This led me to a deep letting go or letting be and the onset of a forgiveness experience so profound that in one fell swoop, all the hurts I'd carried toward my parents since I was a child were gone in an instant. What replaced or came forth in that open space of the heart was a pure love not of me, but from the extraordinary gift of forgiveness.

You see, they were victims of their own hurtful past conditioning and lacked the clarity or benefit of mindfulness and wisdom that gives us a choice in each moment to either follow affection or conditioned anger as the "gifts" we give to others. If you see the pain of your own life with wisdom and compassion, why would you ever give these hurts to another? Ask yourself!!

It is mindfulness with wisdom, compassion, and forgiveness that helped to break this cycle and replace it with an affection that tries to lift up others instead of tearing them down. This is one of the greatest marvels of mindfulness and perhaps our most important work in progress in this life. It was an experience, not done by me, a surrender and cleansing so deep and complete that the anger/resentments were transformed. For the rest of my life, I only had love and the desire to lift up my parents and help them whenever I could.

This was crucial for me and resulted in a complete redemption (to make up for my hurts toward them) and reconciliation (to repair completely my relationship) with them both. Both my parents died, with me holding them as their most reliable and trusted friend. A true best friend. I didn't just love them; I also really liked them. This is important. I have been fortunate to hold many of my "dear ones" as they passed on with a joy for their release and a love that knew they would be in my heart forever.

Please, listen from the deepest place in your heart! Here's what makes forgiveness one of the most important and profound teachers of transformation and guardians of the heart – deep forgiveness in the moment rewrites/transforms that moment and begins to rewrite with wisdom the moments of the "future." Forgiveness allowed me to rewrite the future with my parents in a skillful and kind way for the rest of their lives, transforming my difficult ones into dear ones, another true marvel.

"Forgiveness does not mean ignoring what has been done or putting a false label on an evil act! It means, rather, that the evil act no longer remains as a barrier to the relationship. Forgiveness is a catalyst creating the atmosphere necessary for a fresh start and a new beginning!"

– Dr. Martin Luther King, Jr.

May those of us who read this do the same and smile, as this is a gift available to all.

Our Forgiveness Meditation Exercise

First, settle in and sit comfortably in the body. Do nothing special except relax and smile – you have been given a precious human life, and you are here not by mistake.

*Pause as needed throughout

My forgiveness resolve – May I and others forgive and have forgiveness for all the thoughts, words, and deeds we've done unskillfully out of greed, hatred and delusion, and confusion.

Remember – forgive yourself and others before you walk out of the room!

Like compassion, it is usually important to extend forgiveness to yourself first – as forgiveness comes from your heart, and this can become a gift to everyone you meet in life.

If it doesn't feel right for you, to extend it to yourself first; of course, extend forgiveness to someone else first if you like. Add others in your life over time, and eventually add all sentient beings to your forgiveness practice. Much like loving kindness practice.

With soft attention, breathe gently into your heart space area. Feel if there is any tightness or tension – if there is – relax, but whatever is there is okay!

Now envelope or surround your heart space with a warm, soft attention and find affection if you can! Smile; you have the gift of the possibility of complete forgiveness already in your heart. This is the natural tendency of the heart, along with affection. Smiling softens the heart! In love, there is a natural letting go or letting be, and acceptance of the difficult and maybe forgiveness.

As you connect with your heart, see if you can feel an appreciation for yourself – for doing your spiritual work, for getting up when you've fallen down, and for love, you've given to yourself and others, even if not always returned. For being here and truly showing up. For the courage to walk the spiritual path and gratitude for this precious human life.

Now find something you've done or some way you've hurt or harmed yourself – something manageable, not overwhelming. Picture or remember it.

Now with a kindness and gentleness of heart, begin our forgiveness phrases or make up your own if you like.

May I have forgiveness for those thoughts, words, and deeds which I've done or given to myself unskillfully (out of greed, anger, or delusion). (Say this 3 times)

I can and do forgive myself!

With your words and deep letting go, can you feel the burden of carrying heartaches and pain start to lift? Try to release them through heartfelt forgiveness. I can and do forgive myself.

Remember to add others to your forgiveness phrases as you can and as your heart space allows them in. Eventually, adding all sentient beings to your practice.

Don't rush the process, it will unfold at its own pace.

Try this exercise frequently and use it whenever you judge yourself or others harshly or hurt someone. Begin to remove the pain of your past from your backpack and finally put it down if it is no longer useful! Feel the lightness and relief of letting it go, and smile!

Use our reflections that arrive next. They will lift your spirits.

Reflections for a Skillful, Forgiving Life

Try to accept your common humanity or our humanness. We all struggle, so always be kind to yourself and others. Compassion starts in your own heart and is a gift freely given to others.

Remember the perfection of your imperfections. Images of perfection will only cause you to suffer if not understood and balanced with compassion.

Remember, we can only do the best we can – that is the truth of our life.

Remember, be kind to yourself, be persevering, and smile for the gift of life.

Though it may not be apparent to you, there is a wonderful transformation taking place in each little bit of forgiveness for those unskillful words and deeds in each human life.

Remember, forgiveness is a great gift of kindness for yourself each and every day – forgive yourself as often and early as you can.

Give forgiveness, as the precious gift it is in this life, to others early and often – it will transform this moment and hopefully future moments of your life skillfully in the direction of goodness.

Remember, choosing forgiveness instead of more judgment from some image of perfection is one of the keys to letting go of suffering and sorrow.

Know you are appreciated and loved by many.

Chapter 9

Moving With Clear Seeing to Realignment Beyond the Cushion – Skillful Means

I wish you happiness.

After years of insight meditation and lots of retreats, including three 3-month retreats, I left the safety of Insight Meditation Society (IMS), the safety of the cushion, and all the sangha I'd ever known. Before I left, I spoke with Joseph, who said, "You will always be in my heart." This sent me off with a deep gratitude and appreciation for his teachings and friendship. I also carried a faith and courage that my life realignment would allow me to move in the direction of goodness and truth and, most importantly, be able to maintain my practice and continue to walk the path of discovery. I knew that was crucial for my survival, as was also finding a skillful living.

I knew I couldn't just make money; I had to make a difference and help people, which was one of my first strong realignments on the path! I also knew the importance of service (right livelihood) and meditation. They saved my life, as they can save yours. Remember, the long arms of mindfulness reach and lighten even the darkest corners of your mind and help you find your way with clarity and wisdom as your guide.

I knew I couldn't go back to my life of suffering and felt my spiritual resolve had to be unwavering and sincere. I had to really mean it because there were few sangha members or spiritual support groups that I knew of, particularly in Georgia in the 1970s and early 1980s.

My lifelong resolve had to contain mind factors with behaviors driven by deep intentions, which assured a skillful life of goodness with wisdom and compassion always as my guide. These are many of the skillful means I used then and even now in this precious life.

Skillful means are all the aids we need to maintain not only a mindfulness practice but a skillful perspective and lifestyle for a lifetime. Also, skillful means can support clear seeing, which allows us to continue to hear and recognize the friends, teachers of transformation, and guardians of the heart that arrive in each moment, providing guidance for us all along the way. Skillful means were crucial in helping me each day and will help you survive and thrive in an often chaotic, difficult, and divided world.

Here are some of my most important resolves with actions, which allowed me to maintain my lifelong journey on the path of goodness, discovery, and truth:

Daily Practice:

Have a daily mindfulness (awareness) practice and sit every day for a minimum of 30 minutes, sometimes much more but never less. This was crucial to me and has been essential for following wisdom with clarity and skillful perspective throughout my life. Like eating every day, but this was spiritual nourishment! In the beginning, I was rigid – I tried first thing to sit quietly in the morning and then again in the evening for at least one hour each session, and even more when I was at home. I admit I did have a fear of being overwhelmed by the lack of support around me, but I found quickly that I needed to be much more flexible in a busy householder's life.

During my rigid sitting phase, I went on a trip to Yosemite Valley with a friend. I was adamant about sitting for one hour every morning at 7:30 AM and one hour in the evening at 7:30 PM. One morning at our campsite, as I was meditating in the quiet of my friend's Volkswagen Beetle with the windows closed, two teenage girls walked by. They noticed me and giggled and said something, but I didn't respond, move, open my eyes, or open the windows. Twelve hours later, as the sun was setting on Yosemite Valley, I was sitting again in exactly the same spot, and these same girls walked by once again. I heard one of the girls say in horror to the other, "Oh my God, he must be dead! He was sitting there this morning." I quickly smiled, rolled down the window, and said, "No, I am fine. I was meditating this morning and am meditating now." We all laughed, and I wished them well.

As my practice and equanimity grew, and I became much more flexible, I sat anywhere and anytime, but I still took a no-excuses approach. Be very aware of the procrastination voice that puts off sitting or practice until tomorrow, because tomorrow never comes. Your best intentions are important, but without an actual meditation practice of clear seeing with follow-through, your practice will or may become stale or eventually nonexistent. A student asked their teacher, "How much should I sit?" The teacher replied, "You should sit for at least 30 minutes a day unless you are too busy. Then you should sit for an hour."

Stealing A Moment (Flexibility):

I have used a phrase for most of my life that I call "stealing a moment." It's all about being flexibile and looking for opportunities to be mindful and take silence or the stillness of the moment wherever and whenever you can. That could be on a train, in a plane, at a doctor's office, or while you are standing on the corner waiting for a friend. Most of the world has little reverence for quiet or stillness, so find your own, even in the small opportunities found in each day. They will add up and make a positive difference in your path progress.

The encouragement to do this may not come from anyone but you. Our society doesn't reward sitting quietly and turning inward. Instead of listening to a voice that says, "Don't just sit there, do something!" remember this meditation phrase: "Don't just do something, sit there!"

Pick small things to be mindful of that you do each or most days. Brushing your teeth and washing your face, vacuuming, running, yoga, raking leaves, using the treadmill, and more are all simple, easy activities that are ideal ways to expand your insight meditation and crucial daily practice.

Walking meditation is an extremely important addition to any overall meditation practice and, when developed, is of great daily practice value. It can and will help expand your general awareness to actions you do every day. It can also help you steal a moment of mindfulness and is the perfect way to bring practice into daily life. Initially, use mindfulness with walking at a slow, conscious pace, eventually bringing awareness to the body in all of your daily actions at a more regular pace. I also wanted to mention, as your walking meditation matures, see if you can add a more expanded sense of awareness. This allows you to walk within awareness as opposed to walking with awareness. It provides an expanded or boundaryless awareness which becomes a choiceless awareness including all mind/body objects.

Eating meditation is another practice that brings awareness into your daily life. I always use awareness of the body first for this meditation since it is my ground or base camp to help stay present. It is also super-important for me to start each meal with a food blessing or prayer because it always brings me back to presence. My food blessing is: "May all living creatures share with me the benefits of this meal, and by the power of the Dharma, of the truth, may all beings live with health and happiness. I dedicate this meal and its awareness to the happiness and freedom of all living creatures."

Driving, which many of us do every day, is a welcome addition to expanding your practice. After you turn your radio off, use an expanded general mindfulness of the body so you don't miss stop signs. Your work or any meetings, including family gatherings (which certainly can be stressful), are all possible places to meditate in action. They require and are helped tremendously by finding mindfulness of and grounding in the body.

Grounding in the body is of huge importance for bringing your meditation practice back to the cushion and each moment, as well as to your daily life progress off the cushion. Remember, the body and the breath are always present and are also always in the present moment. They are also both important as touchstones. To be here now, simply return to awareness of the body, and you will find your natural ground practice in the moment! Embody your body, and it will relieve the attachment to living a life only between your two ears.

Nature:

Make a daily resolve to spend a few minutes in nature every day. As a psychologist for more than 30 years, I was constantly around people, their problems, and, many times, their crises. In fact, I worked as a Crisis Intervention team leader for 26 years. To maintain my balance and my ability to arrive at work each morning with fresh eyes for a new day and a true sense of beginner's mind, I discovered that living with nature was crucial.

There is a great power of nature to bring you back to center and awareness of the present moment. Use that to your advantage as much as possible. I made a conscious choice where my family and I lived. To be surrounded by the beauty of nature gives peace and calm to the deepest part of you. This is something we all understand at a deep level. (As a child, my family called me "nature boy" because I always wanted to spend my time there instead of playing with other kids.)

Slow down, listen to the birds sing, leaves rustle, and breathe in the natural beauty. Also, spend some time reflecting and appreciating what we have, like sangha, family, a job, health, loved ones, food, and a roof over your head. Yes, travel the world and kiss the ground when you arrive home in your heart, wherever you are! Appreciate and smile more, complain less!

Dedicating Your Practice:

Dedicating your practice to a higher intention can be part of keeping it fresh and alive. I begin each sitting meditation with, "May I dedicate my life's practice and its awareness to the happiness and the freedom of all living creatures, and by the power and purity of the Dharma, of the Truth, may we all come to a deeper purity of heart guided by wisdom and compassion, to help bring all beings to a deeper appreciation and understanding of loving kindness, joy, and our true heart of natural affection."

Dedicating your practice makes it much deeper, more dependable, and larger than yourself. I remember my practice is for all beings and thus of larger importance and power than my individual fears and desires. I've needed this reflection and resolve many, many times in dark times with dark corners of the mind and life!

A daily resolve is also part of my dedicated practice – "May I be kinder, wiser, more generous, and more aware each day." Do this first thing before you get out of bed if you can, as your day's first wakened skillful activity. And smile.

Loving Kindness:

Loving kindness is the natural affection of deep purity of heart. As the debris of delusion and confusion begins to dissolve, loving kindness may manifest as your true nature. Along with compassion, joy, and equanimity, it is considered one of the divine virtues, or Brahma-viharas – very important friends, guardians, and teachers on our path of goodness.

Developing and maintaining a daily loving kindness/compassion practice is a crucial part of your overall practice. Insight practices sometimes need the warmth and humanity of loving kindness/compassion practice for balance. Wisdom and compassion can get out of balance at times, with wisdom getting too cool (aloof) and loving kindness/compassion getting perhaps too warm without equanimity (for example, a compassionate traveler to impoverished regions of Africa or India might become broken-hearted or overwhelmed by the magnitude of the poverty and the challenging living conditions).

Heart practices also need the wisdom and equanimity of insight practices for balance and perspective. So, my strong suggestion is to always include a metta or loving kindness practice as a part of your insight practice, and vice versa if you primarily do a heart practice. So what are insight practices, exactly? Imagine someone bringing a high degree of mindfulness and concentration to everything happening in the body and mind and noticing that these arising and passing body sensations, feelings, and thoughts are impermanent, not "me" or "mine," and that we suffer when we cling to them. It is best to balance these powerful wisdom practices with loving kindness/compassion. While this balance eventually comes naturally, you can help foster it by intentionally practicing metta or loving kindness.

"May all living creatures everywhere find and have real happiness and freedom from suffering and from sorrow" is a short phrase that contains both loving kindness (wishing for the happiness of all beings) and compassion (wishing for others to be free from suffering and sorrow).

Spiritual Community (Sangha):

The last essential ingredient I'll mention to maintain your practice for a lifetime is the importance of a spiritual community or sangha. This has to be a place of safety and friendship and can be a tremendous support for overall practice and mindfulness for the long haul.

Sangha must feel safe and be safe; a place to be supported and cared for in good times and difficult times. You have to show up and do the work, but it is easier with others. My wife and I went to a sangha many years ago, and when we left, I said, "I don't think those people like each other!" You must feel love and warmth in a healthy sangha even if you do not agree in all things, which you won't. It is important that all are welcome because our heart must have room for whoever arrives! The dear ones and the difficult ones.

It is important to decide ahead of time what you are looking for in your search for a sangha. They can be fairly easily found online, meeting for activities like group meditation, dharma talks, social interaction, book study, or community volunteering. Some are in-person-only, others online-only, and still others, increasingly since the pandemic, use a hybrid model of both (i.e., some members gather in a physical space, while others watch and interact from home via services like Zoom). In-person has the benefit of developing a closer-knit sangha, friendships, and stronger commitment. Online, of course, is more convenient, less labor-intensive, and can also provide opportunities to "visit" sanghas anywhere in the world. If you are looking for a teacher and guidance, choosing a teacher-led sangha would be your best choice. Peer-led with no specific teacher is an option, allowing all members to discuss topics equally.

However, there are fewer controls over mere opinions versus experiential wise view. I have attended all of the above, and each has its own merits and shortcomings. The foundation must be safety, mutual affection, respect, and always guided by wisdom and compassion. It is best to be seen for yourself.

When in community, and in all aspects of your life, remember to smile and use SMILE during the good times but especially the difficult ones. When you practice SMILE, giving your own natural smiles to your local community and the world, you feel safe, and others feel safe around you. This is a big part of our good news story. It will help transform your life and the lives of others as well, a true marvel.

My Wish for All Beings

When things seem difficult, I wish all beings hope and courage.

When things seem chaotic, I wish all beings inner silence and guidance by wisdom.

When things seem complicated, I wish all beings simple beauty and clarity.

When there is sadness, I wish all beings joy and happiness.

When there is illness, I wish all beings peace and protection, with healing, supportive hands, and health.

When there is loneliness, may we be a beacon of love, compassion and companionship for all sentient beings.

Lastly, may the truth guide you; may the truth protect you, and may the truth surround you and all beings with love, kindness, and compassion, guided by wisdom each and every day for the rest of your life!

Be safe, stay healthy, and know you are loved and appreciated!

Part 2

As Life Unfolds

An In-depth Look at

the Dearest Friends of Mindfulness

Introduction To Part 2

As Life Unfolds With Marvels and the Dearest Friends of Mindfulness

Vernon Howard reminds us, "Do not be impatient with your seemingly slow progress. Do not try to run faster than you presently can. If you are studying, reflecting, and trying, you are making progress, whether you are aware of it or not. A traveler walking the road in the darkness of night still going forward. Someday, some way, everything will break open, like natural unfolding of a rosebud."

Although virtually all of this book is about the marvels of mindfulness, the transformations of the whole of our life, it's also important to make clear a few points for wise perspective. Mindfulness or insight practice is not a "quick fix" for all your problems. It took a lifetime of some strong, deep conditioning to get here, so be patient and kind to yourself. But I do know that many realignments from insight and transformation do come along the way. Some fast, some slow, and some I just don't know. Transformation is real and does happen, but wise faith, persistence, and honest diligence are required on this path of discovery to awakening.

If you believe the path will be easy and there are roses in nature without thorns or that someone or something outside yourself can "save you," you may or will leave the path. The truth you seek can only be found in the one that sees and the moment that is now. This isn't negotiable. Smile, this is all part of our good news story.

Chapter 10

The Dearest Friends of Mindfulness and Awakening – Relevance for Practice

Yes, you are loved.

Although you've met some of our friends on the path already, let me introduce all of the dearest friends of mindfulness that arrived to guide and protect me throughout many years and are still with me today. In these next several chapters, I'll talk about what the Buddha called the Seven Factors of Enlightenment. These factors are the foundation for all the teachers of transformation and guardians of the heart, but also, importantly, the dearest friends of mindfulness, which travel hand-in-hand with you throughout your spiritual journey. They are mindfulness, investigation, energy, joy(rapture), tranquility(relaxation), focus (concentration), and equanimity.

The Buddha was asked by one of his monks why he called these the factors of enlightenment. The Buddha replied that these are the seven mind factors (the Buddhist tradition counts 52 in all) that lead to and must be balanced and present for enlightenment to occur. They were also described as the antidotes for all the most common meditation hindrances. This chapter is an overview and the first in a series of chapters on our dearest friends, including their relevance for our lifetime of mindfulness or insight practice.

Mindfulness with its dearest friends have great relevance to our practice for many reasons, but primarily two related to the five most common traditional meditation hindrances. These may impede your progress in establishing a strong wholesome foundation of goodness for your journey.

These hindrances are:

Sense desire/greed – holding on that can drive and control us.

Hatred/ill-will – pushing away from; aversion deeply linked with anger.

Sloth and torpor – low energy and tired, bored, or hazy.

Restlessness – too much energy, difficulty sitting still or focusing, regret/ worry.

Doubt – uncertainty with delusion and confusion (often with fear) also includes procrastination. Both can become dangerous as they can stop or postpone practice.

The first four are very common and are routinely seen often early in practice, yet do still visit again at times. There are many antidotes, but these hindrances are skillfully handled by the most important antidote of being mindful with our friends, teachers, and guardians of the heart. However, additional antidotes are discussed in detail in Chapters 9 and 19.

Also, later I'll discuss an important friend, teacher, and guardian that is crucial to our journey of goodness: doubt guided by wisdom. It is part of what guided my life through my period of angst and urgency that I mentioned in Chapter 3.

As the seven mental factors develop and strengthen, the five meditation hindrances begin to appear less frequently. Our progress on the path speeds up as a direct result.

Secondly, as our friends develop and mature in your meditation, the hindrances weaken and become much more "workable" as your perspective changes. With wisdom and the seven factors of mind, you start to see the hindrances as teachers – lessons for change and transformation. This mind alignment is hugely important because all aspects of life can and will become your teachers and guardians.

Let me explain – it is often our reaction to difficulties through aversion (pushing away) or greed (pulling or holding on to) that paradoxically forms a deeper attachment to the very difficulties we're trying to overcome. Our attempts to escape the difficult many times recondition their return performances and narratives. It all recreates an unskillful relationship with the "unwanted" and an unskillful feedback loop which is more resistant to the healthy change we seek. Fear is a good example, where the more we resist and react, the more it is fed. By contrast, with complete acceptance in the moment, fear is starved of the reactive energy and dialogue it needs to persist and grow. See if this is true for yourself, and you will smile.

Now let's talk in-depth about what I consider to be the most dangerous of all the hindrances from a practice perspective: doubt, guided by delusion and confusion, which is one of the main reasons meditators stall on the path or abandon it.

It is a doubt with hesitation, a lack of commitment, and full of confusion and second-guessing. There is a huge difference between doubt from fear and deluded thought, and doubt from wisdom, which can be a profound and skillful guide. For example, when I graduated from college and found a doubt with wisdom that whispered, "Don't follow others who aren't happy," this changed all of my livelihood decisions and, in turn, the whole of my life.

Doubt from wisdom brings investigation that probes and questions in a silence that "speaks" and says, "Why would you listen to the doubt of fear and delusion from conditioning, that only wants to take you back to a life of suffering and angst that you left decades ago?" With the doubt born of wisdom, you will see clearly the doubt born of fear, delusion, and confusion. Wisdom will say with conviction, "You fooled me before, but not this time." Smile – you are beginning to see!

So let me define and discuss very simply each of these universally important factors of mind.

The first of these dearest friends is mindfulness, which is arguably one of the most important ingredients of our spiritual foundation because it sees, balances, and keeps in check its other six friends. It is awareness that sees and knows without pushing or pulling. Mindfulness with wisdom and wise view guides your development of meditation and the other dearest friends of awakening.

Early in the process of insight, mindfulness naturally brings a second friend called investigation. This is a mind factor with the ability to see the details of the mind/body process clearly, with the probing quality of intelligence. Investigation is a very important wisdom factor of awareness and clear seeing. It includes investigative listening, which is important during all Dharma talks, and deep wisdom listening in general – for example, being present and listening carefully to others.

With investigation and interest/curiosity, you'll notice our next friend – energy – which, of course, is always present in some way. In this reciprocal relationship, interest usually brings additional energy, and energy often brings deeper interest.

Energy is the "juice" that supports all our friends and is the fuel of effort and seeing (knowing). You know when energy is too low (sloth and torpor) or too high (restlessness in the mind/body or both). Mindfulness again balances this friend carefully because energy for wise meditation must be continuous and relaxed. Not too low and not too high – just enough for direct, clear seeing/knowing.

Our next friend of mindfulness is included in almost all meditation practices, even those that arose in India centuries before the Buddha's teaching: focus or concentration. This arises naturally from interest or, often, as a result of a deliberate effort to attain exclusive concentration or samadhi, the ability of the mind to stay focused on a single object or objects to see and learn. Concentration unifies the energies of the mind. It may naturally bring our next two friends: joy and tranquility.

Joy and tranquility many times arrive together and have a strong, sometimes tandem relationship with focus and concentration. Joy can range from just slight ease/happiness (our Mona Lisa smile) to full on rapture. Tranquility can range from slightly relaxed calm to deep abiding contentment, where you can't find a reason to get off the cushion (which you must!).

This brings us to the last friend: equanimity. This is the ability of the mind to stay balanced/calm not just before the "storm" but also during its middle and end. Equanimity is characterized by a balance that comes from deep letting go or, deeper still, moving to letting be. It is full acceptance of the present moment and, just perhaps, love or affection as the natural state of the heart.

These seven mental factors are some of the most important and dearest friends of mindfulness. When they are present and balanced, deep insight/awakening may occur.

The most important thing to remember: Mindfulness starts the process and balances the other six dearest friends. So first, develop mindfulness. As you walk the path, mindfulness will keep your mind clear, knowing, balanced and wise.

Chapter 11

Mindfulness With Investigation

Yes, you are appreciated.

Let's talk a little more in-depth about our first two dearest friends, mindfulness with investigation. Imagine hearing these teachings for the first time, with the freshness and aliveness of a *beginner's mind*. To encourage reflection, I'll ask several questions.

How did your life on the path start? Mine started with a deep, persistent dissatisfaction I couldn't shake, an abiding darkness. My curse, or so I thought, was the sense that nothing was ever good enough and that there was no way out. My mom marinated in dissatisfaction in precisely the same way. She never overcame dissatisfaction, but is it possible to do so? Let's see.

I carried this deeply imbedded delusion (darkness) and all the suffering and pain of that until I heard my teacher Joseph Goldstein ask the simple question, "Can you be aware?" In that moment, I began to see the possibility of accessing a light I didn't know existed – the light of mindfulness, which is part of an unbroken chain of authorized truth, learned directly from teachers going all the way back to the Buddha more than 2,500 years ago. As it began to shine in me, my life gradually began to transform.

Mindfulness is simply the relaxed knowing with acceptance of the current moment. No more and no less. Knowing through clear seeing is enough to take your first step on the path and a new beginning.

Ask yourself, do we truly accept the moment? How often do we change objects and search "outside" of the present moment for happiness? Can everything in your life be a teacher of transformation? Of course it can, if seen and known clearly with investigation and acceptance.

How does transformation occur? It is like turning manure into fertilizer, as mindfulness brings one of its first and dearest friends – investigation – to probe the interplay and interaction of objects, allowing wisdom to arise. Investigation is the penetrating quality of intelligence and is perhaps the main wisdom factor of mindfulness and clear seeing. With interest and energy, we dig in to see the true nature of our mind/body process, asking questions like, *Is there anything solid or unchanging here, anything that truly could be said to be me or mine?*

Investigation also brings interest with curiosity, which unifies the energies of the mind and creates a natural focus or effortless and relaxed concentration. Think of how effortless it is to focus on a good story, universally true teachings, or the silent wisdom of your own deepest insights.

Mindfulness constantly works in concert with investigation and our other dearest friends. It begins to allow wisdom to be found in not only each of the difficulties you face in life but also all of the many friends, teachers, and guardians you encounter. You begin to see choices you didn't know you had, like stepping out of the way of adversity or a poison arrow by opening your heart so completely that there is no longer any target to hit. When you have fewer buttons to push, it creates a tremendous sense of safety for you and others.

What if you said "I love you" more and fought with family or others less? Can we also really like the very family or one we say we love?

"It just seems like we've been mad at each other for so long," says Chelsea (Jane Fonda) to her father Norman (Henry Fonda) in the 1981 movie *On Golden Pond*. "I didn't think we were mad," Norman responds, "I just thought we didn't like each other."

Is there enough affection in your heart for not only dear ones but also the difficult ones? Ask yourself.

So, does mindfulness transform darkness into light? In each moment of mindfulness with investigation, there is a retraining and a natural addition of our other wholesome friends. It's a realignment of the mind in the direction of awakened values such as honesty, integrity, generosity, kindness, and inclusiveness. As this happens, gradually or quickly, all aspects of your life move in the direction of wisdom, loving kindness, and compassion. These are all wholesome goodness factors, some of life's greatest gifts and marvels.

Chapter 12

Energy – Benefits and Dangers

Be patient and relax!

Let's talk about another dearest friend of mindfulness, which is energy, the juice of life! We're told the amount of energy in the universe is constant, incapable of being created or destroyed, and can only be changed from one form to another (1st Law of Thermodynamics). The Center for Astrophysics | Harvard & Smithsonian describes energy and matter as "the two basic components of the entire Universe." That includes us, as part of the universe.

Everything, including the human body, is made of energy, so it's certainly really important. Fortunately, we don't have to understand astrophysics. We can keep it simple and focus on skillfully navigating the energies of our own life, just as they are presented to us in any given moment. So, love, hate, compassion, anger, and joy are all energies with different colors and likely different behavioral (karmic) outcomes if not clearly seen.

Energy supports all the mind factors and is the natural fuel for effort, seeing, as well as path progress. You know very quickly in meditation practice when energy is low, resulting in sleepiness, lethargy, and a foggy or cloudy mind, sometimes referred to as sloth and torpor. You also know quickly when energy is too high: It appears as restlessness in the body, or *papancha* – a busy, unsettled mind.

So, what is the most skillful way to deal with and balance most typical low or high energy states? Of course, the answer generally is mindfulness, which carefully balances all of the other six dearest friends of awakening, including energy.

Nothing happens without energy, which is crucial to our practice (especially our initial effort). However, the energy for wise meditation must be continuous and relaxed – not too much and not too little, just enough in the middle for direct, clear seeing or knowing.

So, does insight meditation naturally increase wise energy used in the direction of awakened values? Again, the easy answer is, "Yes, in a number of ways." But why? Because these wholesome mind factors bring investigation and interest when they work harmoniously together in our practice, arousing and renewing energy. This effortless unification leads to a natural focus, inclining the mind toward seeing and knowing. If you're interested (inquisitive) in something, there is usually a "new" and increased energy present to see and learn. If you're bored, energy is probably low. Why? Because you're likely not very aware. But see for yourself.

Energy also builds as the mind becomes more unified, calm, and focused with behavior and decisions coming from our deeper wisdom (a vital teacher of transformation and guardian of the heart), with less mental division and tension. You're also less burdened by unskillful thoughts, words and deeds during your daily life, which then helps you sleep better and recharge more quickly. Remember, division always burns energy and wears you/the mind out.

As your practice progresses, wisdom will become your guide with increasing frequency. This balances your effort and helps you live a more skillful life. The greater clarity that results from meditation practice also allows you to save energy by handling stress and responding to "adversity" more skillfully, with less energy-sapping friction. All the pushing (adversity) and pulling (greed) wear out the body and the mind and burns up crucial, useable energy for your lifelong journey on the path.

I read an interesting article from the EquiSync Institute with a quote that said: "It's noon, your iPhone has 10 apps running in the background, you have been non-stop texting your beloved, and you had to make an hour-long phone call this morning. Is there any wonder your battery life is at 22%?"

So, there are lots of benefits to continuous, relaxed energy and effort guided by wisdom and balanced by mindfulness. A boost of skillful energy may be one of them.

But what about energies that become too high and can pose a potential danger? This is fairly uncommon from insight meditation during daily practice or outside of retreats, in my experience, but high-energy states can and do occur in intensive retreat environments.

It seems to happen when retreats hold participants in a tighter controlled "container" with increased levels of concentration and an emphasis on more rigorous effort. In my experience, having put in the proverbial "10,000 hours" of retreat time, these retreat characteristics, more often than in other practice environments, also increase the likelihood that participants may struggle with unintended high-energy states and dark corners of the mind.

Over-striving and self-imposed performance pressure, both commonplace, can ramp up these phenomena even more, triggering anxiety, fear, doubt, insomnia, and other potentially challenging states. In insight meditation circles, there's a term for this cascade: a "multiple hindrance attack." Over-striving often results in burnout. You feel overwhelmed and just want to give up. When this happens, it is important to reach out to a skillful teacher for perspective and wise counsel.

Another phenomenon that seems to be fairly rare, but does happen enough to discuss, is the spontaneous release of intense life-force energy or kundalini from the seven energy centers or chakras. This, too, can cause fear and angst if equanimity is not strong. Kundalini energy is usually more referenced in Hinduism than Buddhism and refers to an energy in everyone's body, usually unknown or in a dormant state. This energy is not usually inherently dangerous, and it can actually be very beneficial.

In fact, many Hindu and other spiritual traditions practitioners seek it out and consider it divine. In most early Buddhist traditions, experiencing kundalini energy is not a high priority. However, it is acknowledged that it can be skillfully activated, most often through deep samadhi, and that when mindfulness is present with kundalini, it is considered wisdom energy. Tibetan Buddhism and other Vajrayana lineages may describe this as tantric energy.

Generally, with all very high-energy states, it is prudent to talk with a skillful teacher who knows the importance of grounding and recognizes early signs of difficulty. It is very helpful to use grounding in the body, settling into its contact points in your posture.

For most energy issues, mindfulness will easily balance the ups and downs as practice progresses, along with the other dearest friends of discovery and awakening. Simply being aware is most often the key to maintaining relaxed, balanced energy and effort, important friends of mindfulness.

Chapter 13

Wise Natural Focus and Concentration

Be joyful!

Let's talk more in-depth about our next dearest friend, which is natural focus and concentration. I'd like to give a very short historical perspective of the importance of wise focus and concentration (samadhi) in Buddhism, remembering virtually all forms of meditation contain these mind factors.

Let's start with the Indian prince Siddhartha Gautama, who became the Buddha after his awakening and lived for an amazing 80 years around 500 BCE. Siddhartha's family were what we would today describe as Hindu and probably of the Brahmin or warrior class. As noted by Britannica, "[a]lthough the name Hinduism is relatively new, having been coined by British writers in the first decades of the 19th century, it refers to a rich cumulative tradition of texts and practices, some of which date to the 2nd millennium BCE or possibly earlier. If the Indus valley civilization (3rd–2nd millennium BCE) was the earliest source of these traditions, as some scholars hold, then Hinduism is the oldest living religion on Earth."

Siddhartha's wakeup call was the Four Heavenly Messengers – old age, sickness, death, and a monk walking with a look of serenity and happiness. Siddhartha searched for years for the "Truth" and the end of suffering. He wandered in the forest, learning meditation from very wise teachers. When he had learned what each teacher had taught him, he moved on to another wise teacher.

According to Buddhist tradition, the meditation of the times was exclusive samadhi/concentration, and so these were most likely *Jhana* (meditative absorption) teachers.

Exclusive concentration is a very important component of all insight or mindfulness meditation and many others, including Hindu and Christian forms. Examples include Transcendental Meditation (TM), mantras, visualization, centering prayers, and loving kindness practice. The emphasis is on one-pointedness of mind, undistracted through effort, keeping the mind on primarily one object. It is often called exclusive concentration because it holds to a chosen object (like the breath) to the exclusion of thoughts and other objects.

This concentration provides the power, steadiness, or strength of mind required to stay on an object and see its details clearly. So, it is an important skillful tool.

Exclusive concentration also very effectively brings joy with tranquility to practice. This is sometimes referred to in the tradition as "gladdening of the mind." As the mind unifies its focus and energy, both joy and tranquility increase dramatically and can be useful on the path. I'll talk much more about this in my next chapter.

Exclusive concentration is an important part of meditation because it slows down the mind's bullet train or roller coaster. Excluding objects is very useful up to a point. However, very deep exclusive concentration without the wisdom and clear-seeing of mindfulness can lead to some issues, especially deep attachment, even addiction, to rapturous mind states. In some Buddhist lineages, practitioners caught in this trap are likened to hungry ghosts – mythological beings who become attached to and continually strive for pleasures, in this case altered states of mind. The Buddha was very careful about too much exclusive samadhi.

Effortfully focusing the mind on any one object can create tension, in part because of the object preference or attachment that can develop. (Generally, zooming in on the breath builds concentration, while staying mindful of arising and passing body sensations develops more open awareness). A few years ago, a friend and facilitator from a local meditation group told me he felt tremendous tension when he heard the daily train pass through his town, since he struggled to continue staying on his breath. I smiled and said, "Remember, all objects are equal in their ability to be teachers of transformation and allow wisdom to arise." It is more skillful to remember to be aware of whatever is predominant in the moment. There's no need to attach to any one object as special.

Does concentration alone purify the mind? In my experience, you can concentrate on anything – the internet, your phone, driving home, etc. Concentration is simply a tool. It sharpens the blade, but only wisdom swings the blade to cut the roots of greed, hatred and delusion.

Deep, exclusive samadhi suppresses the hindrances, which can be appropriate and useful, but it does not cut those roots. This is very important –it's the reason the Buddha did not find awakening with his early Jhana teachers.

In Southeast Asia, many teachers and monks teach lots of exclusive concentration in the beginning of practice, often for weeks or months until the student reaches so-called "access concentration." Mindfulness comes only later. What is access concentration, exactly? Most view it as the level of focused energy sufficient to reach or access all stages of insight. However, there are some subtleties here.

Most Western teachers, like myself, teach moment-to-moment concentration and mindfulness *together* from the beginning of one's practice. As a teacher, I have practiced both exclusive and moment-to-moment concentration. Ultimately, though, I have found students will likely come to true moment-to-moment seeing with *choiceless awareness*, where predominant objects are seen with no preference or choice. This awareness includes a natural focus from interest and curiosity with investigation as your meditation practice matures.

The moment-to-moment or momentary concentration used in choiceless awareness is called *inclusive concentration*.

Strongly coupled with mindfulness, it includes all objects equally. If exclusive concentration could be likened to a "blow torch," inclusive has a much softer, more open feel. Objects of mind are allowed to interact freely and uninterrupted.

Nonetheless, there is still a high level of focus and unification of the mind, with interest and curiosity driven by wisdom.

In inclusive concentration with mindfulness, the mind does not hold to a single object but includes all phenomena from the mind/body process without deliberate choice. Inclusive concentration with awareness maintains open attention to the constantly changing flow of all objects. Our life on and off the cushion is seen as the flow and interchange of these mind/body objects. In each new moment, this allows a more skillful transition between the cushion and our activities in daily life. By seeing the natural flow and interplay of objects, the process of mind/body is seen at a more process level beyond content, thus allowing wisdom to naturally arise more readily from interest and curiosity.

How to come to inclusive concentration? Letting go of a singular concentration object, such as resting and being embodied in the body with presence, helps lead to inclusive concentration coupled with mindfulness. I've included a natural focus (inclusive) and concentration (exclusive) exercise, as well as an awareness-of-awareness, moving to choiceless awareness, exercise at the end of this chapter to give you a real experiential sense of their differences. Enjoy!

Concentration Exercise
Inclusive and Exclusive

My intention and goal as a meditation teacher is to help give you the skills to foster transformation in all of your life. The most skillful teacher is not the one who tells you the most, but the one who shows you the most! So, practice with this exercise and see what happens.

A big part of this exercise is to see the difference between exclusive and inclusive concentration.

*Pause during the exercise where and when, as you see fit.

Let's keep it simple – relax and be aware. With effort, direct the mind to the breath at the nostrils and stay there, and if possible, rest on the breath with your full attention. This is exclusive concentration in a very simplistic nutshell.

Since during exclusive concentration, the mind stays on a primary object for a long time, a strong object preference can develop, which can cause tension when other objects arise – car noise, somebody moving or coughing, talking, etc. Also, exclusive concentration constricts the awareness and mind dramatically. Insight and awakening open or expands the mind, it never constricts it. (Remember this!) –

Settle into the breath exclusively and relax.

Now, let go of the breath completely and let the awareness settle into the body. As the awareness and mind expand, notice the objects that become predominant without willful choice – thoughts, sounds, sensations, etc., flow and interact naturally. The "same strength" of high interest focus of mind can be present but with more space and much less object restriction and suppression. Allow the mind to open and expand with a high-interest focus and attention! This is inclusive concentration. See if you get a sense of the mind now resting in awareness, which is also a sense of choiceless awareness, with no or little object preference suppression. Relax, accept, and let be with a soft open awareness – no resistance.

This is part of "letting go of the mind" which is discussed late in the *Anapanasati Sutta*. If the mind gets scattered or loses focus, just come back to your usual (breath or body) primary object. Remember, inclusive concentration with mindfulness sees the whole play, which allows for wisdom to naturally arise from a big-picture view. Exclusive concentration sees a much smaller picture, perhaps only the lead actor or actress you're enamored with, and you may miss the other actors and just maybe more of the story (because you miss the interplay and full view)! See for yourself if this is true, and smile.

Mindfulness/Awareness of Awareness Exercise – Moving into Choiceless Awareness

Although it can be relatively simple to be aware of awareness (or wakefulness), it is quite subtle and may be elusive until it just naturally happens. This is sometimes taught as the last object (called knowing consciousness) in mindfulness instruction (longer retreats) of the mind/body process. It is a very subtle, immaterial object because it isn't seen, it is known.

When I was young and early in my practice, I would try to find the knowing of awareness, but didn't get it at first. I was trying too hard to find something that is there all the time but is subtle and holds the objects of mind I was used to seeing.

Metaphorically – I was looking for the clouds (the objects of mind) instead of the sky (awareness holding the objects). Did you get this? I'll explain as we go along.

We'll try this a couple of different ways!

*Pause during the exercise where and when, as you see fit.

As always, rest in the body first – feel the grounding, relax, and settle in with a smile because the friends, teachers, and guardians will teach as we listen and observe.

Continue to sit quietly (*no* intentional focus on breath – just rest in the body) and begin to let the awareness expand and surround the body. Pay attention to the sense of space from *sitting within awareness.* Knowing of the space you're sitting in is awareness of awareness. Knowing the knowing!

You may also notice this can become a deep natural awareness or knowing, not of you, that the object or objects that are predominant appear in each moment with no preference or choice. This is choiceless awareness as the mind simply rests in awareness. It is what Tibetan schools call *unfabricated awareness* because it arises or is present without effort or a "you" preference.

If you get it, good, if you don't, don't worry, you will. Let's move on and try a slightly different approach!

Now move to sound – see the natural expansiveness of hearing sound.

Sound may lead to the perception and knowing of space.

Now ask, are you aware right now? With a yes, again notice the expansive nature of the mind (Big Sky Mind) – the expanse of space – is it separate or filled with knowing, saturated with knowing/awareness? See for yourself – here is again awareness of awareness or consciousness.

Let me say it another way – it is easiest for me to notice wakefulness as the Big Sky Mind. All objects – thoughts, sensations, emotions are what pass through (the clouds if you will) the vast open space of choiceless awareness.

The knowing of the open space of awareness, the sky, is quite simply the awareness of awareness or wakefulness. Again, notice it is also choiceless awareness: No object is chosen, they just naturally pass through the sky of the mind of their own accord, no effort is needed.

Lastly: Rest in loving awareness as it is your (our) home for life. It is spacious presence, that which sees, knows choicelessly, but is not of you. Smile – it's a true marvel.

Chapter 14

Joy and Tranquility - Gladdening the Mind/Heart

You are a joy!

Let's talk more in-depth about our next two dearest friends, which are joy and tranquility. Remember, we've already talked about mindfulness with investigation, energy, and focus/concentration.

Joy and tranquility allow you to bring light into darkness and help provide a balanced, skillful perspective when things are difficult in your life. Joy and tranquility many times hold hands and often arrive and appear to move in tandem to result in a relaxed sense of wellbeing.

Joy can usually range from just a slight touch of kindness, ease, or happiness (our Mona Lisa smile) to full-blown rapture. Tranquility can often range from slight, relaxed calm to deep, abiding contentment – during some states of deep, exclusive concentration (samadhi), you can't find a reason to do much of anything or get off the cushion.

I would be remiss not mentioning serenity as a synonym for tranquility, since the Serenity Prayer surrounded me growing up. This short prayer from the theologian Reinhold Niebur (1892-1971) is a cornerstone of virtually all 12-step recovery programs. It states: God grant me the serenity to accept the things

I cannot change, courage to change the things I can, and wisdom to know the difference. This prayer helped my dad a great deal with his sobriety. It also happens to be very aligned with our teachings on the path of goodness and discovery. The serenity or tranquility to accept the things that are out of our control is one of the primary antidotes to prevent suffering and leads to freedom from suffering. It is also a larger skillful view of our path that there are many things in life we cannot control, but can be recognized through mindfulness as dear friends, teachers, and guardians along the way.

One of the many important shades of joy is the perfection of heart or brahma-vihara of *mudita*, or *appreciative* or *sympathetic joy*. In its simplest meaning, this is joy for the happiness of others. It's a very specific antidote to one of our greatest poisons in life, and one that was very present in my upbringing, having been passed down through the generations in my family: jealousy. In fact, it took a long time for my mind to align toward a true, deep joy for the happiness of others. In our culture, we generally aren't taught that jealousy, like anger, poisons the heart first and covers up natural joy. As a result, jealousy still runs unchecked in many people's daily lives.

For me, joy often is the gratitude that moves to appreciation for all the lessons of life and the sentient beings in it, especially the difficult ones. Whenever adversity knocks on your door in life, we can with time and practice, all develop our immediate Mona Lisa smile that arises and says, "Welcome, come in. You are accepted and appreciated as my friend, teacher, and guardian." It is a gladdening of the heart/mind that can arise as natural, selfless joy.

Joy and gladdening the heart are important. There are basically two widely used paths to meditation joy. The first is exclusive concentration. As the mind unifies its attention and one-pointedness improves, joy may naturally arise, usually with increased tranquility as well. Both joy and tranquility are largely dependent, in this case, upon specific causes and conditions. Strong, exclusive concentration/samadhi is fairly transient; it's often one of the first factors to weaken as you get off the cushion. See for yourself!

Another path or road to joy, and one which is often more stable and resilient, is *vipassana* or insight joy, based on clear seeing with wisdom. Gladdening or joy can also be part of investigation, bringing wisdom and the important teaching of letting go/moving to letting be and, perhaps, love (more to come).

Also, joy and tranquility are reinforced and supported when commingled with the dearest friend of equanimity. What I think of as equanimity joy says, "Come what may; we're all friends here." With investigation and wisdom, insight with equanimity has a much firmer foundation in the mind and can become a reliable, more stable friend in a difficult human life.

The joy and tranquility I now know most often may have originally been from exclusive concentration, but as practice matured it eventually evolved into insight joy with equanimity and the release from letting be. It's a resting in awareness, an awareness before thought, which contains a deep insight joy and a profound tranquility/contentment born of freedom.

As I've mentioned before, in the beginning of practice, our Mona Lisa smile may not feel so convincing, but with the willingness to keep answering the door of life with acceptance, you will see for yourself that you actually mean the "welcome." This smile naturally arises with joy and tranquility as a heartfelt sense of appreciation for the opportunity to transform the difficult or unwanted into true friends, teachers, and guardians.

Our smile of joy and tranquility is hugely beneficial in maintaining a skillful, balanced perspective in what at times, can be a difficult life. It brings light to the darkest neighborhoods of the mind and your life.

Remember that some of the special sauce or initial skillful action for starting to transform all difficult emotions and mind states is the simple smile of a welcoming acceptance, joy, and appreciation for the opportunity to learn from all of life. It is also the easiest door to access loving kindness and all of the "heart" practices – perhaps surprisingly, the "wisdom" practices, too.

Once your heart has been touched by insight joy, even for a moment, you may notice the smile I've talked about and a natural affection that comes to visit.

"Sometimes your joy is the source of your smile, but sometimes your smile can be the source of your joy ... Because of your smile, you make life more beautiful."

– Thich Nhat Hanh

Gratitude or Joy Exercise

*Pause during the exercise where and when, as you see fit.

Relax – be aware and settle into your body.

Smile – you have been given a precious human life and you're here and can reflect on your spiritual friends that care for and love you. In that care and love is safety. Feel the natural joy that may arise as your heart warms – relax and smile! Feel the tranquility or peace that comes from the certainty of the care, love, and safety our community of spiritual friends provides.

(Reflect on each of the following for a few minutes before moving on to the next one)

Let's move back in time a little and realize in any life it is skillful to reflect on the dear ones that care for you and keep you from danger, at least until you could make your own way. Feel the warmth of joy for arriving on this path safely through the care of many, some you know and some you don't.

Reflect on the gift of a body that still works – perhaps just not as well as it once did – but smile in joyful appreciation for the opportunities we still have.

Smile at the difficulties you've overcome and all of those who stood by you during the rain and storms, and the ones who enjoy the vistas and sunsets with you.

Reflect on the things – car, food, and roof over your head, and the "stuff" of life that make it all possible for you to read this book.

Reflect on the thousands of people that you know and can imagine are responsible for the food, roads, our health, and protection. For the pets, and the people that make you smile and the compassion you have for the ones that don't.

Finally, reflect on the ones (millions and millions) you don't know and will never know but are still deeply interconnected with. Feel the joy leading to tranquility because we work together and do care for each other. Smile knowing you are joyfully loved.

Chapter 15

Equanimity With Patience

I wish you balance and peace.

Our last dearest friend of mindfulness is equanimity, which often travels together on the path of goodness with patience. Moment by moment, equanimity and patience frequently comingle, support, and reinforce each other.

So, what is true patience, both conventional and spiritual? It is the calm, clear recognition and acceptance that things can and will happen in a different way and order than what you thought. It has a quality of enduring or persevering with a skillful perspective toward a life that is full of change. It took me years to finally, deeply understand and accept this truth. Impatience was religiously "practiced" in my home when I was young and is still rampant worldwide. Western society today is speedier and more impatient than ever.

When you are most easily patient, consciously present and mindful, what is present? It is calmness, an acceptance of what is, with equanimity and wisdom.

When we are in a long line, slow traffic, waiting for an answer, email, the computer, or our phone to reboot – all are inherently neutral. However, what often comes from us is impatience, annoyance, anxiousness, all triggered by a desire (wanting mind) for something to be different than it is. To have patience with others and family, take a deep breath, pause and be mindful. Check your heart's true intention before you speak or act! A moment of patience in a moment of anger can save hours or years of regret, disappointment, and difficulty later. Don't react to your first impulse; relax, and pause to allow your deepest wisdom to arise, especially with family and relationship issues.

If you are not patient, what happens? You hurt yourself from your own anger and stress, and more importantly you do the same to others. How often have you given away as an unskillful "gift" irritation or annoyance to those around you? Use wise reflection and see if this is true. Smile – we can and will transform this, with clarity and affection.

As discussed in Chapter 6, spiritual patience allows us to stay the course on the path, no matter what, with a skillful resolve and affection, knowing "this too will change." It's about returning the next day with a "beginner's mind" and restored faith, along with a wise commitment to continue our lifetime of spiritual work for all sentient beings, with gentle perseverance and renewed patience.

"In our busy lives, we may easily overlook the value of patience in our quest for accomplishment, efficiency and fulfillment. When we recognize that seeing, peace, compassion and love are quite different from, even incompatible with, compulsive behavior and reactions, the value of patience becomes apparent. Patience entails choosing not to respond reactively, allowing other possibilities to arise; it provides tremendous support for mindfulness and gentle perseverance."

– Gil Fronsdal

If patience is the calm recognition and acceptance of *what is*, then how do we distinguish it from equanimity? Very simply, equanimity is less about an intellectual or emotional understanding of the way things are; instead, it is a calm balance or evenness of mind where there is no push (aversion), no pull (greed/attachment) – just deep letting go or deeper letting be. From the traditional insight meditation map known as the Progress of Insight: "There will arise knowledge perceiving evident bodily and mental processes in continuous succession quite naturally, as if borne onward of itself. This is called 'knowledge of equanimity about formations.'" To see and let be! It is an even-mindedness that allows you to not ride all the ups and downs of life! Equanimity arises through awareness and, once developed, is one of the most reliable and dearest friends of all the awakening factors. It is necessary for the mind to be balanced for deep insight/wisdom to arise. It works as the ground for and is rooted in insight/wisdom.

Seeing with the balance of equanimity allows the mind to not get caught by whims and what in the Buddhist tradition are called the "Eight Worldly Winds": praise and blame, success and failure, pleasure and pain, fame and disrepute. With clear seeing, there is balance of mind that develops an ability to remain centered in the midst of whatever is happening. Equanimity is not just the calm before the "storm" (although the calm before helps to diminish the storm), but the calm within the storm can be an active factor for positive change after the storm.

As dear friends of mindfulness, the qualities of equanimity and patience help us see and understand the bigger picture – like never attending the fights or disagreements we are invited to, and developing the capacity to refrain from reacting to our first impulses ("Well, I'll tell him a thing or two!"). Instead, equanimity with patience allows us to wait until our deeper wisdom arises, saving us untold regrets. These friends of mindfulness act as a part of the "sacred pause" – that small space or momentary silent reflection in which we can speak and act more skillfully. Remember, none of us is perfect at this; we will make mistakes and have regrets.

There are a couple of skillful phrases I say to myself as reminders. One is "just sit on it" (the email before you send it), and I also use this phrase for important decisions, or life decision quandaries. I also often use the phrase "let's just see" – meaning give some decisions or actions time so you don't react but rather respond skillfully. Deeper wisdom often arises with stillness and patience.

This happens naturally and more quickly as greater wisdom, patience and equanimity translate into more skillful action in all dimensions of your life. This process is active, not passive. It gives you a larger perspective, allowing for skillful responses before, during and after the "storm." Making wise choices in the present "rewrites the future" and softens the past.

All of this is why, traditionally, equanimity (*upekkha*) is considered the foundation of the Brahma-viharas and the greatest jewel of all. Without it, a heart filled with loving kindness, compassion and joy could be overwhelmed by the magnitude of suffering in the world. It naturally balances the heart as it teaches and protects you even during crises.

My 26 years as the psychologist in charge of the Crisis Intervention team (Intervene) for a major Metro Atlanta school system coincided with the progression and maturing of my spiritual practice. Increasingly, I found that my mind became calmer and more balanced even as turmoil, panic, or conflict increased among the people we served (and sometimes team members themselves). It might seem counterintuitive, but it happened dozens of times over the years. It's not something you do but is something that is "done to you" as a gift of equanimity with patience.

Please remember that equanimity is one of our greatest teachers of transformation and guardians of the heart. It is the dearest friend of mindfulness that is largely responsible for allowing the mind to rest in loving awareness and the natural stillness of the unconditioned.

"Try to be mindful, and let things take their natural course. Then your mind will become still in any surroundings, like a clear forest pool. All kinds of wonderful, rare animals will come to drink at the pool, and you will clearly see the nature of all things. You will see many strange and wonderful things come and go, but you will be still. This is the happiness of the Buddha."

– Ajahn Chah

Meditation Exercise
Mindfulness With its Dearest Friends

Mindfulness with its dearest friends are all related, integrated, and naturally supportive of our insight meditation practice. They're all seen throughout our practice as we walk the path of goodness, discovery, and truth.

*Pause during the exercise where and when, as you see fit.

Let's see how this works – smile – this is your precious life, and we are together as you read, reflect, and meditate on these friends.

Of course, we start with mindfulness – so settle in, relax and smile as your first skillful action that says, "welcome." Bring awareness to the present moment, using either the breath or the body. They are apparent, always present, and inherently in the present!

As you settle into the breath or the body or both (as I do), see how the mind and the body start to quiet and settle down. Staying with the breath, body or both with mindfulness is enough!

As mindfulness increases, investigation is aroused, bringing interest and natural curiosity to see and know clearly what is happening in the present moment. Investigation is a primary wisdom factor of mindfulness, and with its interest will see that each moment is new, alive, and ever-changing.

Investigation and interest bring renewed energy and a natural focus (effortless unification of mind – important). This is a natural relationship and happens with all interest containing inquisitiveness. When you're interested in something, see that you will likely discover a natural energy and focus toward the seeing or the doing.

As energy is aroused and balanced by mindfulness, your natural focus may improve (see if this is true). Stay here for a minute or two to strengthen this mind factor.

Deeper focus (breath or body preference) will often lead to one of many joys, as the mind becomes more unified. Maybe soft and silky, or a stronger real sense of happiness with joy. A unified mind, as we discussed, is one of the major ways to bring forth joy.

As our joy naturally relaxes the mind and body, we move into tranquility. A contentment or deep relaxation, a kind of well-being.

Tranquility and joy are often mixed and can lead to deeper relaxation and focus, but of course deeper natural focus also commonly leads to a deeper sense of tranquility and joy. They naturally support each other as friends.

With mindfulness, investigation, energy, focus, joy and tranquility working together, we arrive at equanimity – a deep, balanced letting be. An equanimous mind allows the full unfolding of whatever is in the present moment. It also provides a safe refuge for you and others, and, just possibly, a gift of affection for all beings.

Finally, remember that mindfulness with wisdom starts the process toward discovery, goodness, and truth. Mindfulness is the "great protector and balancer" of all our dearest friends, helping them to remain your reliable trusted companions throughout your precious human life. Smile, you really do matter and are loved.

Lastly, rest in loving awareness as it is your home for life.

It is spacious presence which sees, knows, but is not of you. It was present before you and will be present after you.

It is your friend and protector for life. It will not fail you and will bring many of your dearest friends along the way!

Smile.

Part 3

Additional Friends, Teachers of Transformation, and Guardians of the Heart that Arrive Along the Way

Introduction To Part 3

Additional Friends, Teachers and Guardians that Arrive Along the Way

No matter what you've done or where you've been, you have been chosen to walk this path of goodness. You're not here by mistake, and you do matter.

Life always gives us the teachers we need, but not always the ones we want. Smile when you answer the knock on your door of life. A heart of affection will help to transform you and maybe even a "difficult" visitor!

I have seen thousands of people come and go from the path over the years. Some found another practice – I hope – but many got caught by the "distractions" and pace of life. Some left for a while, and some left for perhaps a lifetime.

I truly hope you thrive as you resolve to be kinder, wiser, more generous, and more aware in every aspect of your life. I also hope the many friends, teachers, and guardians I've talked about will continue to help the truth guide, protect, and love you each day for the rest of your life. Smile; this is all part of our good news story for having a skillful, wise, and compassionate life.

This path can be one of joy, compassion, and of loving kindness, but it can also be a challenging, difficult path at times (my early story). It requires resolve, persistence, commitment, and of course, the warmth of good spiritual friends!

The good news is that our greatest source of difficulty: reactive pain (the 2nd arrow, as covered in Chapter 2), can many times be reduced completely. How? By the clear seeing of mindfulness, with the balance of mind from equanimity and the wise perspective from wisdom. This is the profound teaching called freedom *from* unnecessary pain, as the mind remains clear, balanced, and unmoved with wise view and wisdom. This is real, extremely doable, and available to each of us in every conscious moment. See for yourself. This is one of our most important gifts and marvels on our journey.

If you do happen to fall, get up and try again. The world, with its seductions, will pull you away from the path and tell you there are more useful and important things to do. There aren't! Know what you must do and continue to walk the path even in the face of opposition, distraction, and obstacles, no matter what. If you persevere in this way, you will find support from additional friends, teachers, and guardians that will make a profound difference between quitting or moving skillfully forward. In Part 3, we explore some of these supports and how they arise from and relate to the path: the relationship between wisdom and compassion; the precious gift of discovering compassion through forgiveness; the essential roles of generosity, morality, gratitude, and appreciation; and the critical importance of fully transcending the "us-and-them" mentality through unconditional love.

On the practical front, we investigate antidotes and skillful means for dealing with challenges that can arise on the path, as well as the potentially tricky "far and near enemies" of the Brahma-viharas. Finally, in conclusion to Part 3 and the book, we look at the transformative power of engaging in even deeper spiritual inquiry: Is there truly a locus of control? What is the role of thought in meditation? What is psychological time, and does it have any reality? If we radically accept the deep truth of inclusivity, what are the implications for our life? We also present a further exploration of SMILE as a support to practice.

Our spiritual work has to be done, is more important than ever, and is the most beneficial work of our precious human life. Smile; there are many more marvels to come!

The Guest House

This being human is a guest house.
Every morning a new arrival.
A joy, a depression, a meanness, some momentary awareness comes as an unexpected visitor.
Welcome and entertain them all!
Even if they are a crowd of sorrows, who violently sweep your house empty of its furniture, still, treat each guest honorably.
He may be clearing you out for some new delight.
The dark thought, the shame, the malice.
Meet them at the door laughing and invite them in.
Be grateful for whatever comes.
Because each has been sent as a guide from beyond.

– Jellaludin Rumi

Chapter 16

Wisdom and Compassion

You warm my heart and bring a smile to my face.

Wisdom and compassion are two of the most important friends, teachers of transformation, and guardians of the heart, along with mindfulness, which are also crucial parts of our spiritual foundation. These both, of course, begin to arrive fairly early in practice. However, because of my extreme angst and difficulties, went largely unnoticed for a while. So, let's discuss them now as they provide extremely beneficial lessons in our life all along our path.

For meditation to be full and balanced, we need both the expansive perspective that wisdom and insight practices provide and the open-heartedness (with loving kindness) that arises from compassion practices. Insight or mindfulness practices lead to unfiltered, clear-seeing – the necessary factor for wisdom and, ultimately, awakening. Seeing begins the freeing.

Without a heart practice, such as compassion or loving kindness, our wisdom practice could lead us to become aloof and disconnected from others. Compassion (with wisdom) understands our undeniable interconnectedness and brings warmth, love, and meaning to what can appear as a little planet floating in and surrounded by cold, dark space. Wisdom, through insight, understands suffering, but compassion makes it clearly understood that all living creatures suffer. Yes, I suffer, but also all beings suffer, and we're all in this together.

When I was young, I sat extensively for some years, and I developed more wisdom than compassion. I understood inherent change, the sense of not-self, and suffering/unsatisfactoriness deeply in my own life. However, I lacked some of the deep sense of interconnectedness that comes with an equal complement of compassion with loving kindness.

I could, for example, let go of pain, but didn't clearly recognize the full pain in others or even some of the consequences of my own behavior. It was, "I could let go; why can't they?" I felt distant, not so connected at times, and didn't really get what other people went through in everyday life.

These types of blind spots are commonplace in all religions and paths of discovery and can even enable unchecked abuse by spiritual leaders or teachers. A disconnect between both wisdom and compassion, where the "crazy" wisdom had much more of the "crazy" part than the wisdom part, made this a particular problem in some lineages in the 1970s and '80s. Even today, some leaders and community members seem to have forgotten the moral component of practice and the importance of compassionate, skillful behavior. Yes, it may be empty (not permanent) phenomena flowing along, as wisdom says, but that is not complete unless we remember in a relative sense that we're also suffering sentient beings – that we matter and are wholeheartedly engaged in a balanced, skillful, precious life. Dedicated insight meditators become adept at noting and knowing the arising and passing away of the continuing flood of body sensations, feeling tones, mind states, and thoughts—sensory data, in other words—but isn't a hungry baby actually so much more than just color and noise?

As compassion grew, I could feel my practice "thaw out" and become much more integrated. I saw "emptiness" and stillness, but I also understood deeply our undeniable interconnectedness. From there grew compassion or affection with wisdom, where my path became a dedicated practice for the happiness and freedom of all sentient beings (a *Bodhisattva* path).

A practice that is larger than yourself and dedicated to others increases your resolve. Adyashanti calls it "unconditional follow through": *I must see this through for the benefit of all beings*!

Eventually, for me, wisdom and compassion became balanced. The mind had finally integrated them so that compassion and affection with wisdom arose in tandem; compassion became the action of wisdom, and vice versa.

This brings a fuller, richer understanding of life. Mark Van Buran says it's "like a wave, finally remembering that it's the entire ocean! With this realization, it sees clearly that each independent wave is not a separate entity but rather a temporary rising and ceasing of the same salty water that makes up the whole of the vast sea. When we realize we are not separate from everything else, we may experience the suffering of others as if it were our own. When this happens, the natural response is the wish to alleviate suffering in any way we can, even if it's a simple Smile or non-judgmental, compassionate presence."

Wisdom helps us to see deeply what we are, and compassion helps us to see what we are a part of – the whole human realm or the whole of conscious existence. Said another way, the eyes of wisdom see that what we take to be a permanent self is, in fact, more like a stream or streams of ever-changing phenomena. Whereas the heart of compassion sees you as part of everything and, importantly, that we all matter as sentient beings.

So how do we develop both wisdom and compassion in our practice?

For me, every part of my practice is dedicated to the real happiness and freedom of all living creatures. I always add to each sitting both clear seeing (awareness) and a time for compassion/loving kindness practice. These have been crucial ingredients in my life since I came to the path of goodness. Wisdom and compassion are your birthrights; come claim them. They're free to all that walk this path with diligence and sincerity. Come see for yourself and smile.

"When we are motivated by compassion and wisdom, the results of our actions benefit everyone, not just our individual selves or some immediate convenience. When we are able to recognize and forgive unskillful actions of the past, we gain strength to constructively solve the problems of the present."

– The Dalai Lama

Compassion Through Forgiveness
Caring for Yourself and Others

Relax and smile!
Use reflection and deep contemplation here!
*Pause during the exercise where and when, as you see fit.

May I be kind to myself and others, knowing kindness is the key that opens our heart.

May I give myself the compassion that I need, knowing self-compassion is a gift we can give to all we meet.

May I learn to accept myself as I am, knowing we are all a work in progress.

May I forgive myself knowing we all struggle, which becomes part of our strength.

May I be patient and realize that the quest for perfection is often the enemy of progress.

May I know love and kindness are always possible for myself and others along the way!

May I never have to look far to find goodness, reach far to find love, or search farther than my own heart to find contentment, commitment, and compassion.

(Add "you" and "we" when appropriate.)
And remember:

Loving every human being is *not* the same as loving every human doing!

Chapter 17

Generosity and Morality

Smile, you matter!

Generosity and morality are two very important friends, teachers, and guardians necessary to walk and progress on our journey. Generosity is often the entry point or way to the whole spiritual path, according to the Buddha. It is the beginning virtue of the heart which wishes to help all beings become free from suffering and to awaken.

The Dalai Lama says: "Giving material goods is one form of generosity, but one can extend an attitude of generosity into all one's behavior. Being kind, attentive, and honest in dealing with others, offering praise where it is due, giving comfort and advice where they are needed, and simply sharing one's time with someone – all these are forms of generosity, and they do not require any particular level of material wealth."

I grew up in a household where greed was very prevalent. My mom controlled the money and had a very tough early life. Her stepmom counted squares of toilet paper that she and her sister used. Her household was very stingy, and she was asked to leave her home at 14 years old. This greed, at least some, was passed down to me and my siblings. So, I struggled in this area and had very little practice with generosity at home.

I recognized I needed lots of practice in this area as I changed my livelihood life plans from moving into greed to moving toward generosity. My mantra was service, service, and more service to help all beings. It's why I became a psychologist. On some level, I knew that the antidote to greed is always generosity. I needed to make a difference, not just make more money.

I married my wife Veletta, who needed virtually no generosity/purity of heart work. Her parents both have tremendous generosity from their Christian faith and will do almost anything to help others.

When I was young, I was only marginally generous and way too analytical in my giving. I remember being on a subway train in New York City with a friend back in the 1970s. A panhandler walked into our car. In my analytical way, I told myself he was a drug addict and that I would just be enabling him by giving him some money. My friend and I were both poor at that time, but my friend quickly gave to him. When I asked why, he replied, "He asked for money, and I have a little, so why not? I really have no idea what he'll spend it on. A need arose, and I gave, that's all." I smiled and thought, Yep, he's right.

Now I rarely miss an opportunity to be generous. I also always carry extra money to be ready to give if needed or to help where I can. The antidote for me is "give and walk away," a useful saying I learned that has served me well.

For many years, Veletta and I have continued to work at the Friendship Table feeding program for the needy at our local church many Tuesday nights and the Red Door Food Pantry most weeks. These have been wonderful ways to give back to those in need. Give back for free, and you'll find a warm heart and a valuable smile!

"You must give some time to your fellow man (and woman). Even if it's a little thing, do something for those who have a need of help, something for which you get no pay but the privilege of doing it. For remember, you don't live in a world all your own. Your brothers and sisters live here too."

– Albert Schweitzer

A word of caution. Enabling can be where some of the most generous people I know slip. A common example is overdoing for our children who are "helped" too much and thus can cause conditions for a "failure to launch" and not thrive independently on their own.

Mindfulness also brings a natural morality. Here more generosity, harmony in livelihood, skillful speech, patience, honesty, and inclusivity for all starts to come together in all parts of your life. Morality is not unquestioning obedience to a list of rules, but it is rather an understanding of the effects of karma and the importance of living a life of non-harming and right harmony.

Remember, the five main precepts from the Buddha are to help live a kind, skillful, and wise life. They are based on non-harming and purity of intention, and these are:
- No killing intentionally
- No stealing or taking what is not yours
- No sexual misconduct
- No misuse of intoxicants
- No false or malicious speech – gossip, etc.

Perhaps the three "biggies" in morality/right harmony that we need to give extra attention to are our skillful speech, action, and livelihood. Most people struggle with issues around skillful speech, in particular.

I sometimes reflect on the following questions before I say or respond to someone, particularly during intense, inflamed situations with "difficult" people:

Is it true? The truth is always good, but is it always good to say? I sometimes need this reminder.

Is it kind and not harsh? Generally, no brutal honesty. Ask yourself what is in your heart. Check your heart for motivation and true intention. It may be true, but are you pointing it out to help or hurt? Don't rub stuff in! Truthfulness is an important part of the path, but "be sweet," as my wife tells me. Remember to also ask yourself, What is in my heart that keeps us apart? What divides us?

Is it timely? Is now the right time to say it? (If someone has a problem – don't tell them about yours).

Is it purposeful? This is the most difficult for the majority of us. Idle chatter, gossip, etc., fall into this category. Sometimes the wisest speech is none. Don't attend all of the squabbles you're invited to or go to all of the debating matches that come up (politics). Most all of us need a reminder in this area, for sure.

A friend of mine told a story about keeping an honesty log. Every time he said something, even partially untrue, he wrote it down. When his boss came into his office to discuss something, my friend told a slight untruth, so he pulled out his honesty log.

When his boss asked what he was doing, my friend told me, with forgiveness and compassion in his heart, that he had actually lied to his boss about what the book was for! But telling me about that was very honest. It made me smile and laugh. Honesty is always good whenever it arrives.

When it comes to honest speech, subtle questions such as whether to tell "little white lies" to protect others can be particularly challenging. The questions I have outlined above can help you make the wisest and most compassionate decision. The day my dad was dying, I answered the phone, and it was a relative who was complaining about him. When I got off the phone, my dad asked if the relative was complaining about him. I paused and said, "No, they called to check on you and to say they love you." I have never regretted my decision.

After hurting someone, the most skillful action I have found is to ask for forgiveness and do it before I leave the room. Doing this will lighten your load in life. Skillful harmony with generosity and morality makes your whole meditation practice easier. It allows you to travel your path of goodness wearing a light backpack with less remorse and guilt.

"Just as treasures are uncovered from the earth, so too are virtue and right harmony from good words and deeds. To walk safely through the maze of human life, one needs the light of wisdom and the guidance of virtue."

– The Buddha

A Story for Reflection

The story of two wolves is a Cherokee Indian legend illustrating the most important battle of our lives – the one between good and bad within us. Here is how the story goes:

An old Cherokee is teaching his grandson about life.
"A fight is going on inside me," he said to the boy.
"It is a terrible fight, and it is between two wolves. One is evil – he is anger,
envy, sorrow, regret, greed, arrogance, self-pity, guilt, resentment, inferiority, lies, false pride, superiority, and ego. He continued, "The other is good – he is joy, peace, love, hope, serenity, humility, kindness,
benevolence, empathy, generosity, truth, compassion, and faith. The same
fight is going on inside you – and inside every other person, too."
The grandson thought about it for a minute and then asked his grandfather,
"Which wolf will win?"
The old Cherokee simply replied, "The one you feed."

Chapter 18

Moving Away from Division Into Unity – 'Us and Them' Has Got to End

You are loved!

This will be a discussion full of questions, some answers, and lots of room for mindful contemplation and inward-looking. A good news story of quiet reflection of our life, your life!

Our fears, anger, and greed, as well as all kinds of thought patterns rooted in delusion/confusion, can divide us, but through love, compassion, forgiveness, and yes, our willingness to get along and belong to one another, we can discover and promote unity in this world. Use this discussion as a means to investigate your own conditioning with the clear eyes of mindfulness. These are difficult times. How should we respond? My intention is to do what I can to uplift people and situations by "walking the talk," offering practical suggestions for living life with compassion and wisdom and bringing a skillful, balanced perspective.

What is in our heart that keeps us apart? Do we have room in our hearts for everyone, even those we "don't like" or disagree with? Can we begin to remember we are far more alike than different? If we can't do this, and keep magnifying our differences, then we have failed at what is our birthright – which is to live a life of compassion, affection, and care for all beings, not just our chosen few. A life dedicated to the happiness and freedom from suffering for all living creatures.

We are all part of the world community, and we have a lifetime responsibility every day to help each other and to lift up others when needs arise. That includes all beings, *not* just the ones we like or who think like us.

As I've said many times over the years, "'Us and them' has got to end." As a society/world, we are divided by race, religion, gender, politics, and more. But if we know that we're far more alike under the skin than different, and if we see the disharmony and pain that these divisions bring, then why do we remain so divided?

In the human realm, greed, anger, fear, and delusion are what often drive so much of our conditioning in subtle and obvious ways. Can we be transformed, or will we be swallowed by our own conditioning? Ask yourself!

Delusion and confusion are the main, underlying causes of our separation and division. Delusion leads to attachment to our opinions and views. My dad loved to joke, "Don't confuse me with the facts; I have my opinions." We cling to our views as though everyone should immediately see them as unquestioningly correct. In reality, views and opinions are very deeply conditioned; they are also ever-changing throughout life.

The problem is attachment to "I'm right, you're wrong," and the rest of "You just don't get it." We often surround ourselves with only those who agree with us (just look at the impenetrable "bubbles" that form on social media as people "unfriend" those who don't think and believe like them). Not only does this separate us, but it also begins to harden and close our hearts. See if this is true for you!

But here is the important question: Who is the better teacher, the person you get along with who sounds just like you, or the person who pushes and reveals your buttons? Who is more likely to help you see how and where your heart is still closed and divided?

Attachment (greed) or clinging to view almost always *requires* that we oppose someone of a different view. This division, as with most divisions that are clung to, very frequently moves into anger and aversion, and it may even harden into hatred. In that moment when the heart is closed, you have walked off the path of awakening (I didn't make the rules). See for yourself if this is true.

Can we be a refuge of safety for ourselves and others if our heart is guided and deluded by anger? When the conditioned reactions of anger, aversion, and hatred are triggered in us, aren't we more likely to make things worse by shooting poison arrows back at others? When something happens, and a conditioned reaction arises in us, without mindfulness, we could end up giving a potentially dangerous and destructive "gift" that we deeply regret.

Who suffers first –you or the "other" to whom you just offered that gift of anger? When you pick up a hot coal and throw it at someone else, you will always burn yourself first. Without forgiveness, you'll just pick it up again and again.

In almost anything, pursuing "perfection" or permanence in view can be a fool's game, so be careful. As we noted in Chapter 3, the mind, like the whole universe, is ever-changing (anicca). This is a universal law and is perhaps one of our first teachers of transformation. Attachment to changing objects of mind or views will result in suffering or *dukkha*, which is perhaps our next teacher of transformation, and very often leads to anger. Your anger at others with different views or opinions will only lead to discord with the very ones we often care about the most, like family! We must agree to disagree at times and love each other in spite of our differences, knowing it's OK!

Even our supposed "factual news" we hear these days is often incendiary and used to divide us. What is reported and how is often also based on greed to get more clicks on the internet, for example. Unfortunately, this is because "bad" news, many times, "sells" better and is watched more than "good" news. Go figure!

Ask yourself, would you be angry without anger? On a good day versus a bad day at work, a car pulls out, and our reaction is different, but the car pulls out the same! Ask yourself if you have a date with anger, does it ever take you to a nice place? No, so break up with it. You know it and see it, so let's put the phone down next time anger calls or, better yet, don't pick it up. My saying is, "Don't attend any of the fights you're invited to!" But do we listen *or* do we go to the next invitation?

Let's investigate more closely another part of delusion and confusion that keeps us apart. Regarding fear, the Buddha said, "You must be a refuge to others," and to be a refuge to others, you must have a fearless resolve to see through and make peace with fear. To be a refuge, you must be a place of safety for all beings. But that doesn't mean you should never experience fear. Deeply biological, fear is bound to occur. The key is to not allow yourself to be guided and divided by it – and that requires learning how to work with fear in a mindful and balanced way.

At the same time, fear can actually be beneficial as a protector from actual harm, like from hungry bears! When I was 22 years old, I hitchhiked with a friend for six weeks through several western states. One night, we ended up at 11 PM in a backcountry campground at Yosemite National Park. We set up a tent in the dark. Less than an hour later, as we tried to sleep, we heard two grown bears fighting within inches of our tent. I had an incredible fear of being injured or dying, so I stayed completely still and made no sound. Fortunately, the bears just went after our food, not us. The deep, biological fear I experienced told me in no uncertain terms, "Stay quiet and don't move!" It may have protected me.

Look into your fear. Does it help you or hurt you? Is it rational or irrational? Has it simply been triggered by thinking about something fearful, even something that is unlikely to happen? If we are not careful and mindful of deep fear, it can box us into a dark corner of the mind. We fear many things. In my life, most of the things I've feared have never actually happened. Reflect on your life.

So, what is the key to transformation?

The absolute key to beginning the ending of delusion and confusion (the cause of division and conflict), is mindfulness. Mindfulness is crucial to recognizing all intentions, but particularly the mixed ones and the not-so-skillful ones.

Remembering and staying aware of mixed and ever-changing intentions can be challenging, but it is critically important. For example, your desire to help someone else may be mostly pure, but if it also is mixed with a continuing desire to be "right" and an ongoing attachment to giving someone you regard as "thoughtless" a piece of advice that you are certain they need, how skillful are your actions likely to be? Will they be well-received?

Intentions have to be seen or known to be understood. Only then can we let go of (or let be) those that are unskillful or harmful. Mindfulness allows a sacred pause: With a split-second silent reflection, we can respond skillfully with wisdom instead of reacting from old, unskillful, conditioned patterns.

Mindfulness is the light that exposes our dark corners of delusion and confusion. Remember, mindfulness is the necessary factor for wisdom; wisdom is the necessary factor for the ending of delusion/confusion and ultimately opens the door to skillful action in all areas of your life.

Because there are many times the mind doesn't see clearly and deeply, we believe we are separate and free-standing. We fail to see that we are deeply, fundamentally interconnected at the very core of our being. It is also a universal law that can't be changed.

Lastly, this is important, can we begin to profoundly recognize that we are far more alike than different? If we can do this, and keep from constantly magnifying our differences, then deeper wisdom can and will arise with the keys to what is our birthright – living with compassion, affection, and care for all beings, not just our chosen few. Do we have room in our heart for everyone? If we do, the "us and them" naturally comes to an end! This is a true marvel.

Loving Kindness Meditation

Go ahead and get comfy, close your eyes, and relax.

*Pause during the exercise where and when, as you see fit.

Smile – we have an extraordinary opportunity to see and learn from our dearest friends, teachers of transformation, and the guardians of the heart.

We are born with the capacity for a heart full of affection for others – we just have to do our spiritual work. To see clearly, allowing wisdom and compassion to begin to transform our conditioned tendencies of greed and aversion from delusion and confusion. These cover up the natural tendencies of the heart and mind with what is an affection that *is* inherently your true nature of goodness.

Remember our resolve to come to a life of affection and compassion guided by wisdom, with the clear comprehension that our practice is always for the totality of sentient beings. Smile with freedom from division as you move towards unity.

Chapter 19

Antidotes and Skillful Means for the Common Hindrances

"Life has taught me the wisdom of moving toward what scares me."

– Pema Chodron

Let's talk about some specific antidotes and skillful means suggestions for the most common meditation "hindrances" and other difficulties along the way. These will all likely appear in most any insight or goodness spiritual path.

In the human realm, greed, fear, anger, and other difficult visitors often drive our inner and outer life in subtle and obvious ways. Can we be transformed, or will we be swallowed by these products of delusion, confusion, and our unskillful conditioning?

There are lots of skillful means and antidotes, but for most issues, mindfulness and letting go will lead the list.

Greed or Attachment to View:

Greed underlies most of what we call desire. Desire drives and controls us, making us believe "I just have to have that" and that we will be miserable if we can't get it. But have you noticed that when we do get that coveted object, we are only temporarily happy? It gets old or damaged, or we start to long for a newer-model car, TV, cell phone, etc. Because we are only temporarily satisfied, there is no end to this greed-based desire. A case-in-point: "shopping therapy." We seem to feel better for a while, but then our temporary sense of satisfaction fades, and we have to do it all over again. It's a great example of impermanence or change.

The problem with desire/greed is that its strength/energy pulls us into fantasies, debating, and storytelling – all of which pull the mind out of the present moment and into the past or future.

TV commercials are a perfect example of how greed operates. (It always seems to me that everyone is better looking and having more fun than I ever had!) Isn't consumerism all about amplifying our greed to encourage us to buy whatever is being sold?

Be mindful and reflect. Is desire ever fully satisfied? Will physical beauty remain? Will we lose it all in the end? Remember to practice restraint and moderation; this is the *Middle Way*.

Notice how greed drives you to act, to protect your opinions and beliefs, to "hold your territory." Hear and feel how angry you may get when challenged, which is related to how attached you are to your own thoughts and ideas. This is a very deep and compelling conditioning for many of us.

Wisdom and compassion always win if they have time to come forward – so be patient! Wait it out before you react; it's just another energy that drives you. How many times do you see something differently an hour or two, or a day or two, or much later? There is a huge difference between wise view with a skillful response and an unwise attachment to view with a conditioned reaction. Come see for yourself, and know you can do this one step at a time.

Fear:

As always, be aware/mindful. Many things are scariest when it is dark. Mindfulness is the light of seeing, which allows freeing. Catch fear as early as possible, before it completely fuels or refuels and grows to be "unmanageable." If fear is present, relax, accept it, and find the body with mindfulness.

"Turn down the volume" and "tease apart." are two phrases I often use as skillful means for fear and other difficult energies. Fear can be most intense when we have gotten lost in a compelling and convincing "scary movie" of the mind. These phrases help me remember to turn the music down or off and to tease apart the individual frames that make up the display. Drop the emphasis on thoughts or at least pay less attention (20 to 30%) to the dialogue and the rest (70 to 80%) to the feelings of fear in the body. Use a soft, spacious focus (awareness) on the feeling of fear in the body. Practice this, and it will help loosen the grip of fear, starve it of its fuel, and perhaps, transform it altogether.

Fear's power is largely the power thought gives it. It can't harm you. Met with mindfulness, it can become a valuable teacher.

The conditioned response to fear or anxiousness becomes less powerful and often weaker each time it arrives if it is seen with a welcome and a smile. Ultimately, it is possible for there to be acceptance and letting go or letting be on the first recognition of fear. However, because fear is so deeply conditioned in our biology, it will likely always visit us at some time, to some degree. You can do this, but practice!

A cute story. Don't run, as fear will chase you. When I was a very small child, a large collie jumped on me, pushing me down. It really scared me. Remembering that event, I ran from every dog I met for years – and they all did the same thing in response: They chased me. A few years later, my cousin got a collie puppy named Scamper. She was small and cute, and I had no fear or running. Six months later, I went back to visit my cousin, and a big collie appeared, and as I ran through the house, it chased me. Finally, it caught me after I stopped running, and to my surprise, it was Scamper. She was so sweet and friendly to me. She became my friend for the rest of her life. I also never feared or ran from any dog again.

Let's also talk about two very common energy-based hindrances.

Sloth and Torpor:

Low energy in meditation can show up as tiredness, sleepiness, or mental haziness. We nod off and, if it persists, give up. This is a common phenomenon in retreats, especially in the early morning or after lunch.

Use standing meditation and walking meditation, if possible, to arouse some energy. Other antidotes are going outside, changing your posture, opening your eyes and leaving the breath, and staying with the body. If this low energy happens often, then vary your daily meditation time of day and, remember, best not to sit after eating. If none seems to work, go to bed, get some sleep, and try again tomorrow. Smile – it's OK!

Restlessness:

Here, there is too much energy. Restlessness can appear in the form of papancha – our thoughts are all over the place. These could be from worry, regret, planning, etc. Too much caffeine can also cause a lack of focus or a busy mind.

My wife looked at me once on a 3-hour plane ride (we have done 10 hours with no problems) and said, "I think I'm going to scream." Restlessness can cause all kinds of reactions, so mindfulness is needed as the first antidote.

If you are experiencing restlessness, it can help to walk around, move, stretch, or exercise to burn some energy. If sitting, use the breath and focus or concentrate with an emphasis on letting go of energy/stress on the out-breath. Concentration can bring relaxation and tranquility.

Now back to Veletta's situation on that plane ride. After taking a few minutes to walk up and down the aisle and stretch, she was able to sit down with a restored sense of calm. She had used mindfulness to respond rather than react.

Doubt and Procrastination:

These are deeply embedded parts of delusion and confusion. A doubt from delusion (often with fear), not wisdom, is generally thought to be the most dangerous hindrance of all. Doubt can cause hesitation, a lack of commitment, or something more serious. It can be an impediment to all practice/meditation because it can halt/stop practice. Doubt and procrastination color all thought in practice in the direction of stopping, causing us to say, "It doesn't work," "I can't do it," and ask, "Why am I here?"

Here again, turning down the volume or teasing apart the dialogue can make all the difference. Bringing soft attention to the feelings in the body associated with doubt will help to move the seduction of the story out of the way. The body is not the primary verbal storyteller, but it is always present. Use mindfulness of the body as your ground and a gateway to equanimity.

Give it time, and be patient. Relax and smile, knowing, "Here we go again." You need an unwavering resolve so you can be mindful and never give in to doubt and procrastination. Don't buy or pick up what the mind or feelings of the body are selling. Ask yourself, "When else will it be easier?" As we get older, it is *not* easier with an aging body. Better to do it now, in the here and now, and be present!

Anger:

Anger can range from annoyance and irritation to hatred and ill will. It is often based on frustrated desire, and it can be a very dangerous hindrance. How many people have been hurt, and how many lives have been destroyed by anger? It can cause endless regrets, irrational acts, and unintended consequences.

Anger is always a 2nd arrow. Something happens, often out of your control (the 1st arrow), and we get angry. Road rage and domestic violence are serious examples of how harmful our reactions to anger can be. While driving, someone pulls in front of you. If you're having a good day, you might hardly notice or even wave the driver in. If you're having a bad day, your wave at the driver might turn into a different gesture entirely. Anger can and does control us if we are not careful.

Anger can be dangerous: What initially "feels right" brings fear and regret and burnt bridges later! It can also lead to verbal and physical violence if not kept on a leash. Always try to bring awareness/mindfulness to anger as early as possible. This is crucial to not feeding it. Don't get caught in its web and hurt yourself and another.

Practice restraint by not taking the "bait" when a family member or coworker throws it out, hoping you will bite. Cultivate gratitude and generosity, especially toward those you are angry with or tend to "push your buttons." Both gratitude and generosity soften the heart and can allow us to give that softness as a gift to others. I especially like the phrase "love to you," which can always be used and repeated to help soften the heart.

Know your triggers. Settle into the body and make resolves before you get to work or a family gathering. My birth family was good at throwing out juicy bait on a big hook. Remember, bite, and you get hurt as well as perhaps others. I always meditated before I walked into my parents' home. This allowed me to settle, relax, and ground in the body before the first hook was thrown my way.

Resolve and set an intention to get along. Look at the bigger picture of hurting yourself and others; in an argument, is there ever a winner when there's always a loser? Forgiveness of you and others before you leave the room is an important way to help rewrite your future with wisdom. Use small acts of kindness toward yourself and others; do something nice for someone you struggle with or just someone struggling. Know yourself and let awareness do its job. It will guide and protect you.

Although each of our paths is uniquely different, the good news about the progress of insight from our mindfulness practice is that with clear seeing, delusion begins to gradually dissolve into wisdom. With wisdom and acceptance, anger begins to dissolve into spiritual courage/confidence. As mindfulness with its dearest friends continues as your companions of goodness on the path, greed in all forms moves more easily into generosity with joy. The lessons of generosity and joy begin to overcome anger. Less anger allows the uncovering of our natural affection of the heart. If your resolve is strong and your intentions continue to move toward goodness, you may find that wisdom and compassion were always with you. You just needed your smile to invite them back home. This is also part of the many marvels of mindfulness.

Fear Exercise
Using Smile Into Smiles

Get comfy and stay with relaxed alertness!

*Pause during the exercise where and when, as you see fit.

So, we are going to do a guided practice meditation using anxiety or fear. We'll use mindfulness and reflection, as well as use some helpful strategies to deal skillfully with one of our most painful and powerful emotions.

Thought, combined with fear (which often brings doubt), is one of the most toxic cocktails in life and meditation. This pushes us to safety that is not really safe or healthy (relationships, etc.) many times. Combined, they can also be one of the most dangerous hindrances in meditation progress.

During our guided meditation to help skillfully deal with anxiety or fear, we'll use our newest acronym, SMILE, as a skillful means to help turn all adversity into an opportunity for spiritual growth.

We all know fear, how it feels, and that although it's deeply biological, it is also almost always a 2nd arrow. When something happens in life that, from our deep conditioning, we don't like or want, fear often arises as our reaction, not as a skillful response.

Because we must be a safe person to be a refuge to others and because fear at times can be so harmful and dangerous, we need a strong strategy, so unskillful fear never gets a firm footing.

Our strategy is SMILE which leads ultimately to SMILES and has six steps. The S is for a smile with surrender, M is for mindfulness, I is for investigate, L is for let go or let be until you love, and E is for equanimity or balance of mind, which leads to engagement with our final letter S for safety (a crucial part of our total acronym SMILES). You must be safe to engage in the world community, the world sangha.

So, let's get started – find a small, manageable anxiety or fear of yours to practice with. That could be a spider, dog, mouse, public speaking, heights, person, thing, situation, or whatever you can bring up safely. You know yourself; don't bring up someone, thing, or situation that could trigger overwhelming fear. After you've practiced awhile and progressed far enough down the path, perhaps the "overwhelming" part can be addressed.

Relax and settle into the body and notice the energy of fear in the body. Recognize, accept, and feel it in the body, which is always present. Notice the feeling tone. The body is always the base camp and ground in meditation – use it often and wisely.

See how fear feels in the body, watch its movement, the ebb and flow of body sensations, and how it colors the mind. The body is not a primary verbal storyteller; just the mind's content seduces and sends the 2nd arrow! Don't buy the story, or it will follow you wherever you go and take you where it wants you to go. Smile – it will be OK!

S   Now comes the S in SMILE, which is to have an actual soft smile (Mona Lisa). This will help the early surrender into this moment with fear. This is a surrender from strength, with an attitude of acceptance that "you can't hurt me anymore"! This also does not mean giving in and giving it to another. In the first instant of this soft smile, feel the sea/see change that reduces the anxious aspects of fear because it says, "Welcome, come in, my friend fear. You are accepted and appreciated as my teacher."

M   This smile and attitude change allows you to naturally come to the M in SMILE, which is our soft accepting mindfulness. Allow mindfulness to arise as early as you can before any painful "aspect" of fear is given to another, to see fear with acceptance because it's there and can be a teacher. Smile – wisdom will begin to teach you now because mindfulness will …

I   Bring one of its dearest friends, investigation, which is a wisdom factor of clear seeing, and the I of SMILE. Investigation will work to see how fear can harm you first and can poison and harden your heart with aversion toward something or someone. Fear is designed biologically as an important protector, but if not dealt with wisely can certainly impede a skillful life. Smile; you can make friends with fear.

Investigation will bring you to the question: – would you be fearful if you weren't afraid and to the L in SMILE, which is …

L Let go or let be until you find love (our other L) in your heart again. Love will more likely come as letting go becomes the much deeper letting be. Fear can and will fade quickly if not fueled by storytelling – with affection or soft joy, you will smile naturally and easily. The natural state of the heart is affection, but it can so easily be covered over by anxiety or fear if they are not accommodated or made friends with early.

E You are also now ready for the E in SMILE, which is equanimity that will arise as a natural balance of mind/body since there is deep letting go or letting be, which moves into love. Equanimity from letting be until you love, and love until you let be, bring our other E, which is engage or engagement.

S You can engage again – why? – because you and everyone around you are now Safe (our last S), which turns our SMILE into SMILES. You are safe because you've found wisdom, love, and equanimity again in your heart. You are also, most importantly, a safe refuge for all beings. Bring your smiles and SMILES to the world community because you now have a beautiful gift to give to everyone you meet!

Chapter 20

Is There Relevance of Locus of Control to Our Spiritual Path?

Marcus Aurelius said, "If you are distressed by anything external, the pain is not due to the thing itself, but to your own estimate of it, and this you have the power to revoke at any moment."

What we could think of as "locus of control" is the degree to which individuals believe that they control the outcome of the events in their lives, as opposed to external forces beyond their control. A person with a strong internal locus of control often believes that the outcome of most events or issues in their life derives primarily from their own beliefs, actions, etc. Put simply, it is the belief that "I have the ability to change the course of my life and my destiny."

But are our views and perceptions of locus of control relevant? Do they affect our lives? What about the spiritual path? These questions can get complicated conceptually, as fate, karma, and external/internal locus of control can sometimes wear the same perfume, but the simple answer is, yes, to all of these! So, let's see how.

A person with strong external locus of control often believes that external factors or fate control their life. My life could be determined by my birth, gender, parents, friends, or grandparents. In my case, for example, that meant developing a belief that I had no choice but to go into business since generations of Gebert males had always done this. I had a sense, at least initially, that my destiny was largely controlled by the footsteps of the many before me.

So how do you see your life? The Buddha was fairly clear on some of this, as what happens to us or who happens to us (sometimes the 1st arrow or aspects of external locus of control) are many times not of our choice. We all have an assortment of parents, grandparents, siblings, and other relatives that influenced and conditioned us from our first breath onward, as "fate" would have it. There was no choice in this, that I made, at least that I know.

Most of the world would likely be thrilled with what "benefits" overall I was provided with, again as fate would have it, including education, cars, money, etc. – the American dream. I had a strong sense that external factors had determined the course of my life and believed that my happiness depended on what others thought was best for me.

I had faithfully followed the prescription for happiness that was given to me with good intentions by others, but for me, it just didn't work. I also had a lifelong, deep, abiding sense of dissatisfaction, which I had no tools or understanding of any path or solutions for.

Sometimes everything you're given, including the conditioning for happiness that works for others, just isn't good enough or right for you. Do you hear anything about yourself here? I couldn't follow in the footsteps of anyone I knew – no family, no friends, nobody. All I knew was, I was in trouble and miserable, and no one could help me.

So again, as fate (a concept related to external locus of control) or desperation (a motivator connected to internal locus of control) would have it, I left home and found the simple teaching, "Can you be aware?" With that simple phrase (and some explanation), there was a "sea/see change," a mental realignment from helplessness and hopelessness to a lifelong resolve and purpose to understand the teaching – freedom *from* suffering!

With that realignment, I went from having a strong sense of being controlled by external factors to a deep and intuitive understanding of my own path. I came to know that, in the present moment, there was always a choice and that the sum total of my actions in the moment would determine how I lived my life. This awareness through wisdom changed everything. I could do this! I found a spiritual path that was well-worn by seekers of the truth and many others who also had lived with the "curse" or "gift" of dissatisfaction. (For now, let's Smile and put aside the question of whether there was really an "I" that did any of these things.)

When your feet are firmly on the path of awakening, there will be a dramatic shift from external locus of control to internal locus of control. You will see that the walk is yours. You have a map of goodness, but the journey is up to you, not the spiritual friends, teachers, guardians, and others who help you along the way.

Here's perhaps the most important teaching from a practical life standpoint: Whether you've sat for a week or a lifetime, you can choose to blame the world and many in it for your problems, or to change and live your life with clarity, affection, and compassion, through awareness with wisdom. This critically important shift can happen at any age. A teacher friend once told me about a 93-year-old man who had benefited after coming to sit for the first time with her sangha. Smile, we are in our own good news story.

Yes, of course, you have a right to suffer if you choose, which I feared was my only choice many years ago. But there is another way: the path of discovery and truth. This spiritual path has lots of bumps, detours, and obstacles along the way. Yet, if you persist with unwavering resolve and honest sincerity, you may come to a transformation of heart and mind, which is as fresh and alive as it was for those who walked this path thousands of years ago. If you follow in their footsteps in earnest, goodness is yours for free.

Locus of Control Meditation Exercise

Sit for 5 minutes and do nothing.

* Pause during the exercise where and when, as you see fit.

(Don't get used to this because it won't last for long.)

No meditation – just mindless sitting, no techniques.

Daydreaming, senseless thoughts, and planning are fine – just sit.

This is external locus of control – a life guided by conditioning and more conditioned "fate" meandering toward old age, sickness, and death; in a boat you have very little control over, named SUFFERING and few or no navigation tools.

Now – "Can you simply be aware" – bring mindfulness back!

Notice the sea/see change – the internal locus of control – what allows You the choice to suffer or not. Please, choose not!

In this moment, you've climbed into a different boat named FREEDOM, headed to a safe shore called AWAKENING, and freedom from suffering. The navigation tools are complete, including wisdom and compassion. You just have to have the resolve and sincerity to complete the journey to the other shore. You'll be surprised to know you already have friends and a home there. Come see for yourself and smile.

Take a few minutes to reflect on this exercise and write down your thoughts. Smile, you've done great!

Chapter 21

The Far and Near Enemies of the Brahma-Viharas

Know you are appreciated.

Most of you who have been around Buddhism or insight meditation for even a short while may know of the Brahma-viharas. They are called the Four Perfections or Purities of the Heart, and all very significant friends, teachers, and guardians on the path. These important and sought-after awakened values and heart/mind qualities are:

- loving kindness (metta)
- compassion (karuna)
- sympathetic joy (mudita)
- equanimity (upekkha)

Loving kindness or metta is most accurately defined as a universal, non-discriminating affection or caring for all beings (living creatures). It is an affection that transcends like and dislike – with metta, you can easily have love for someone you may not agree with or whose behavior you may not approve of.

When compassion or karuna is present, we feel the pain and suffering of others as our own. As Mother Theresa says, "We do belong to each other." The connection and empathy of karuna color the heart and mind with a wish to alleviate suffering and the causes of suffering. The heart becomes tender; this is a heart softener.

Sympathetic or appreciative joy, or mudita, is simply the joy for others' happiness. It is a joy that says, "I'm truly happy for you," and delights in the success and happiness of all beings – not just the ones we like. We want joy for them, just like ourselves.

Equanimity or upekkha is the balancer within the storm and acts as a foundation for the first three Brahma-viharas. With this calm balance of mind, there is no push (aversion), no pull (greed/attachment) – just deep letting go and acceptance.

Let's talk about the "other side of the coin" of the Brahma-viharas, or what we call their "far enemies," which separate and divide us as opposed to increasing our connection to life and all beings. The far enemies can and will cause great pain and suffering – and seriously impede progress on the path – so it is important to have an open and honest discussion about them.

The Far Enemies:

The far enemy of loving kindness is hatred – anger and ill-will in all its forms. When we pick up a hot coal to throw at someone else, we always burn ourselves first. Anger was a huge part of my early life and still comes to visit at times, but I know to drop it as quickly as I can, to recognize it as one of those things in our hearts that keep us apart.

The far enemy of compassion is cruelty – purposely hurting another living creature through word or deed. Be aware of the role that thoughts play here. Even when telling someone something "for their own good" or "to be truthful," look at your intention. I had lots of hurtful examples when I grew up. Don't take the bait and hurt someone even if they try to hurt you!

The far enemy of sympathetic joy is envy. It includes everything from minor resentments to more intense forms of jealousy to actually finding "joy" in someone's misfortune. Sometimes words and thoughts can be at odds. We say, "I am so happy for you," but then think something like, "They told me that just to show off or brag," or "They don't really deserve it." Look with mindfulness to discover your true intention.

The far enemy of equanimity is craving – clinging desperately to what we want or aversively pushing away those things we don't want. Equanimity balances all things, so it isn't that craving, clinging, and pushing things away are the opposite. However, when we are identified with and unmindful of craving and clinging, equanimity won't arise.

In fact, none of the far enemies can function as teachers and a skillful part of the path if we are habitually giving away or internalizing them without mindfulness. As I've said many times, we know better than to give these to another as "gifts" because the karmic and negative effects on our lives, and those around us, are too great. But to be clear, they will happen and are always challenges to be aware of each and every time they arise.

The Near Enemies:

Now let's talk about the near enemies of the Brahma-viharas. These shadowy factors or states of mind and heart can be harder to see. They masquerade as the true Brahma-viharasbut subtly create fear and division if not recognized and realigned. They can be seductive because they do resemble the actual Brahma-viharas, which are wholesome and rewarding.

The near enemy of loving kindness (universal selfless affection) is selfish affection – the different energies arising from attached or conditional love. Watch your mind's reaction to this critique of the conventional view of love – do you judge, push back, or accept, etc.? When strings are attached, can fear and clinging be far behind? Look at how nasty divorces can get among people who previously "loved" each other, at least for a time.

Our society has a lot more work to do in this area, which can always be more rich soil for growth. No need to despair; we can just do our spiritual work, recognize the seeds and sprouts of love that we have, and smile.

The near enemy of compassion (feeling a person's suffering or pain as your own, with connection) is pity. Don't get too hung up here. To be sure, the concept of pity is not all bad; the problem comes when we're "feeling sorry" for someone but with a distance in our heart: "Oh, that poor person." Can you see how pity, in many cases, is without a deep connection or the wish to alleviate pain? Sometimes, feeling sorry for someone can be the early sprouts of compassion growing. Is there pain in your heart for others or condescension? It's an important distinction.

The near enemy of sympathetic or appreciative joy (happiness derived from seeing someone else's joy) is a comparison with judgment, which separates us (do you see a trend?) and moves into jealousy. This leads to all kinds of problems – think of them as separation ailments – in our relationships.

I was so glad when this part of my practice and life moved into a universal joy for anyone's success – without the thought of whether they were "deserving or not" based on the judging mind. There was lots of jealousy "in the air" when I was raised.

The near enemy of equanimity can be a little tricky and, in meditation practice, can be seductive or confusing. This is indifference or callousness: A person may look to be equanimous, saying, "I'm not attached, and it really doesn't matter what happens since everything changes anyway. So, who cares!" Equanimity is balance of mind, not disengagement, which can easily slip into fear, withdrawal, and separation.

Indifference (don't care) is different from disinterest (I lost interest in drinking decades ago) and dispassion (I lost the desire to go into business). Do you see the difference? Look closely because this can be subtle. In my youth, while I had discovered equanimity through meditation, I still cared about my values and the way others would be affected by how I lived my life. Yes, I needed to make enough money to live, but I didn't want my livelihood to be primarily about money. I wanted to make a difference, and this was skillful and wholesome.

On the other hand, there was some craving and clinging, too. I did not want to leave my serenity of mind and the protection I had experienced at the Insight Meditation Society. I was scared of the world I came from. Fear was dividing my life between "in here" and "out there" in society. But true equanimity does not contain fear and withdrawal from the world. It allows you, with each step on the path, to have an ease of heart and more balance with the unwanted, the disagreeable, and the unloved, but also with the wonders of life.

Skillful Means and Antidotes for the Far Enemies:

None of us is or will ever be perfect, so we have to have compassion and use forgiveness for ourselves and for others if and when we get caught or seduced by any of the far enemies. Both self-compassion and forgiveness are a huge help in lightening your backpack for the long journey on the spiritual path. A light backpack makes you more nimble when moving out of the way of the poison arrows (hurtful words and deeds, etc.) sent your way.

A light backpack also allows you to make more progress more quickly because you carry less baggage from the past, worry, and regret! Baggage and regret are always backward-looking, keeping you in the past and, many times, causing you to miss the present.

The far enemies are always driven by and arise from greed, hatred/anger, and delusion, called the Three Poisons of any path of goodness. Of course, only one poison is the basis for greed and hatred, and that is delusion (including confusion). It's a lack of right or skillful view from wisdom and compassion.

Not seeing clearly, with only limited wisdom, is the fuel for delusion. Each moment of clarity diminishes delusion by allowing wisdom and compassion to arise. Awareness or seeing clearly is the main antidote for all of the far enemies. Let's talk about this in greater depth to broaden our view.

For hatred, ill will, or cruelty (part of hatred), the antidote is affection or love (with a dose of forgiveness). Only love ceases all the many colors and expressions of hatred/animus, which can't coexist in the same moment as affection. From moment to moment, hate conditions more hate; love conditions more love. It's a simple, universal law.

Hatred, ill-will, cruelty, and jealousy always come from separation and conditioned division. A mind that understands deeply "we belong to each other" will naturally begin to let go of these unskillful separation ailments.

Jealousy and resentment come from a comparing mind and from the mistaken belief that joy and love are limited rather than the awakened alignment that knows that the more joy and love are given, the more there is to give and receive. Reflect on this, and see if it is true! It is true!

For hatred or ill-will, cruelty, jealousy or resentment, and all forms of craving and clinging, mindfulness is always and will be the key to clear seeing, which is the key to awakening wisdom. Wisdom with compassion is the factor that will help cut the roots of the greed, hatred, and delusion that ails all sentient beings.

It is important to remember that seeing is freeing, and forgiveness, compassion, and affection for all will arise naturally as you take this long journey on the path of discovery and awakening. See for yourself! The far enemies are all "bad neighborhoods" and should always be entered only with your dearest friend and protector, mindfulness.

"Men often hate each other because they fear each other; they fear each other because they don't know each other; they don't know each other because they cannot communicate; they cannot communicate because they are separated."
– Martin Luther King Jr.

Skillful Means and Antidotes for the Near Enemies:

None of us is or will ever be Perfect with a capital "P." It's important to have self-compassion and use forgiveness for yourself and others if you get caught (which you will) or seduced by any of the even more subtle, near enemies. The more you see and move forward as you develop a sense of interconnection for all living creatures, the weaker all the "enemies" will become. While the far and near enemies are all part of those "separation ailments" mentioned earlier, they are also important teachers when they visit, so long as we meet them with mindfulness.

Transforming the near enemies and far enemies allows you to realign toward goodness for the whole of your life. This important work is how you begin to change the world. This is perhaps one of our purest gifts – embrace it as a true marvel.

Lastly, as we practice goodness and purity of heart, choose love and kindness instead of attachment, compassion instead of pity, joy instead of negative judgments, and equanimity instead of indifference. Let's learn to open our heart with a smile and accept the truth of each moment, whatever it contains. Remember, the whole of life, if seen with a skillful, wise perspective, is full of teachers of transformation and guardians of the heart, always dedicated to the happiness and freedom of all beings.

Chapter 22

Be Here Now – But How?
Is Psychological Time Real or an Illusion?

I hope you are well and happy.

Time and its implications for our lives are extremely important, and we become friends, teachers, and guardians in helping our transformation. A deep understanding of time can and will change your life significantly if it becomes yours. Listen, but simultaneously see for yourself if what I say is true (Investigative listening)!

On my desk at work, I had a reflection: Always remember – it is the present slipping by us while we're reminiscing about the past and worrying about the future. Many of us habitually miss the present moment in this way.

We'll answer several questions, including:

How to be here now?

Can any object of mind or body be experienced outside of the present moment?

The past and future – how are they created?

Is psychological time real or just a mental construct?

As you recall, in 1974, in my college dorm room, I had a book by Ram Dass titled Be Here Now. I had no clue what being here now meant, but I knew suffering from loneliness, separation, deep attachment to the past, and a deep fear of the future, and I was lost as to where I was headed. After I graduated from college, I went to Naropa Institute and met Joseph Goldstein, who asked, "Can you be aware?" My journey truly began in earnest at that moment.

I began to develop the tools with mindfulness to look at my loneliness and separation (I had left my friends and all I knew). I saw the pain from my deep attachment to the past and fear of an unknown future. Here is what I've found to be true, but see for yourself.

How to Be Here Now?

The easiest way is to simply reside in useful touchstones of the practice, the most common of which are the body and breath. If I had understood early on that these objects are easy to find, always present and always in the present, I would have suffered much less.

But of course, because of the pull from the past and future and a lack of awareness/mindfulness, we only occasionally touch the present (in nature, sitting quietly, etc.) We spend so much time between our ears and believing the movies of the mind.

But wait…

Can Any Object of Mind or Body be Experienced Outside of the Present Moment?

What do you think, but more importantly, what does experience tell you? Conscious knowing is always in the present.

Any object can only be known in the present moment. You must see this for yourself!

So, can any object get out of the present moment? Only if mindfulness is absent and the content of thought is believed and seduces the mind! "I believe the movie of the mind, and I'm in the past or future." But this thought is in the present moment. It is the content that is about the past or future, which is simply a believed image or mental construct.

All objects – including thought, even with content – are in the present moment if seen clearly. What does this mean? The mind must be free from (not of) thought, see it without attachment, and use it as a valuable tool (for example, you might need thought to find your car, do a job, etc.).

The Past and Future – How are they Created?

In an absolute sense, they're created simply by a lack of clear seeing of thought through what we call memory. Thoughts believed as a true depiction of the past "pushed back in time" (illusion) or "pushed forward in time" (illusion) are just craftily created depictions. Importantly, they are always and only offered in this moment (the present).

Are you with me? Thoughts of the past and also the future are part of memory. The past is always a re-creation (not always accurate) believed as true and recreated each time "you" (thought) bring it up. The future is totally made up using what you already know and is an invented "projection" playing the odds – what I think will happen or how I think it will be later – that we fall for and believe.

Years ago, my wife and I went to Costa Rica. My fantasy or mental projection was that it would be sunny, warm, and light outside when we arrived. Instead, it was pouring rain, chilly, and dark at 5 PM instead of 8 PM. Lots of fear came up. We were in a new country at night, and it wasn't what we had expected. It worked out great, but we were worried.

Because we largely live our lives at a relative level, these projections are often necessary and useful. We need them to skillfully plan and manage our lives. Absolute insights free us of the bondage of the "past" and our illusion of what the "future" might be.

Absolute-level teachings allow us to put down our heavy baggage and carry a light backpack on the spiritual path. Letting go of non-useful parts of the past and not believing everything the mind says about the "future" is super-important for maintaining a skillful perspective and responding with wisdom, not our reactive conditioning.

Interestingly, the time of the watch, chronological time (measured by change) occurs and is not in question. You look in the mirror and you know the body has aged/changed. However, the nature of all psychological time and whether it is real or just a mental construct must be examined by you, by us.

Is any psychological time real, or is it always created by thought (a mental construct) for consistency, security, and "self-protection"?

Of course, we create and attempt to conform to an image ahead of a future event – as measured in minutes, hours, days or years. "Here are the things I need to do now to be in sunny Costa Rica on Saturday."

That makes practical sense, but the past is a different matter. We hang on to it for all kinds of crazy reasons – to make us feel better, worse, happy, sad, depressed, etc. We play the same mental tape of all kinds of horrible stuff and somehow, on repeat performance #22, we think it will change or be different. Our daughter watched the movie "Titanic" at least 15 times and cried at the end each time, somehow hoping the ending would change. It won't, but smile anyway.

Remember that every time you "look back" too much, you miss what's in front of you and what needs to be dealt with in this moment. Every time you look too much to the future, you again miss the rich aliveness of the present. See for yourself.

When you know the movie of the mind by heart, when you've watched those scenes from every angle and learned what you can, why not softly turn off the projector and let them go? This will allow you to be here now, in this moment, which is all you have, and continue to move in the direction of wisdom, compassion, and affection for all.

Meditation Exercise (15 or 20 Minutes) For 'Be Here Now – But How?'

Let's see for ourselves how we create a past and future and ask whether psychological time exists apart from thought.

*Pause during the exercise where and when, as you see fit.

We'll start with mindfulness and investigation (the wisdom factor of clear seeing) to see or know the nature of thought and if the past and future are recreated and held onto by thought, thus creating what appears to be "real" psychological time.

Rest in the body, as if it is a chair at the movies. Let the body relax and act as a ground – no more.

The movie of the mind – thoughts and images have already started – because the movie waits for no one.

Let's start with the past. Generate anything about your past. Does your past (5 seconds ago, 5 minutes ago, or 50 years ago) always require a present thought with a recreated thought believed?

Can you get to the "past" without a thought in the present?

Observe without judging or "feeding" the thought.

Can it ever be more than a believed picture (with added narrative) in this present moment?

Now follow the same basic process as above, but for something in the "future," which is even shakier because it hasn't even happened.

Notice how we take info from the "past" and project entirely to this present moment to create a movie about what is to come, based on our learned perspective about the "odds."

Thich Nhat Hanh says:

"You must be completely awake in the present to enjoy the tea.

Only in the awareness of the present can your hands feel the warmth of the cup.

Only in the present can you savor the aroma, taste the sweetness, and appreciate the delicacy.

If you are ruminating about the past, or worrying about the future, you will completely miss the experience of enjoying the cup of tea.

You will look down at the cup of tea, and the tea will be gone.

Life is like that.

If you are not fully present, you will look around, and it will be gone.

You will have missed the feel, the aroma, the delicacy and beauty of life.

It will seem to be speeding past you. The past is finished.

Learn from it and let it go.

The future is not even here yet. Plan for it, but do not waste your time worrying about it.

Worrying is worthless.

When you stop ruminating about what has already happened and worrying about what might never happen, you will be in the present moment.

Then you will begin to experience true joy in life."

Chapter 23

Thought in Meditation
Friend or Foe and Does it Have to Go?
(Anatta and More)

You warm my heart.

This chapter is designed to challenge what you "think about thought." Bringing awareness to your relationship to thought, experientially from clear seeing, has a skillful place in any meditation practice. It can be important to understanding the dearest friends, teachers, and guardians that appear on our journey of goodness and discovery.

Can we agree that all objects in the mind/body "universe" are equal, have the same nature, and are defined and designed by universal laws? They all are subject to change (anicca) – arising from stillness, staying for a while, and ultimately passing away into stillness. They are all the result of causes and conditions which are mostly not under our control. If they were, we'd simply stop thinking when it "interferes" with our practice. Of course, we can't, and it may surprise you to hear that thought is not the enemy.

In fact, freedom from (not of) thought is crucial to understanding anatta (emptiness of a permanent self) and may just be the most direct path to deep transformation or awakening. Let's see why as we continue to see for ourselves!

Whether we believe it or not, because all things are impermanent – deeply subject to change – a solid permanent self with a capital "S" is inherently not possible (anatta). Therefore, all objects are also equal and subject to the same universal laws, whether we like them or not.

But we're conditioned humans, so of course, unfortunately, the answer is never entirely that easy, on most anything. So, let's look at thought. All objects of the mind or body are equal in their nature and ability to allow wisdom to arise when understood. However, because thought takes such preeminence for us, we tend to be much more deeply attached to it in both meditation and life. This can be true even of those who have been practicing for many years. But when we come to understand thought from direct seeing, this has huge implications for maintaining a skillful perspective. In fact, it's at the heart of true, deep liberation. It is largely this object, thought, that is responsible for the belief in a permanent, capital "S" self. Thought is often viewed as one of the major impediments to a quiet or still mind and path progress.

J. Krishnamurti said, "The self is a problem that thought cannot resolve. There must be an awareness which is not of thought. To be aware, without condemnation or justification, of the activities of the self – just to be aware – is sufficient."

"If I could get rid of these darn thoughts, my meditation would be great, I just know it." Let me be the bearer of good and bad news. The bad news – you'll never get rid of thought – it's what the mind does, like saliva in the mouth. It can and will quiet down and might even disappear for some time, but thought always says, "I'll be back."

The good news is, you don't need to get rid of thought. It's part of the mind/body process in human life. So, let's go back to my first question: If thought has the same nature as other objects, like the body, why do I not see that? Because thought can't see its own true nature. You can think about it for the next three years or lifetimes; only awareness can see thought and all objects clearly with wisdom. Through awareness, their nature can and will be known as practice evolves.

Part of our deep conditioning is a hierarchy of thought. Because we are so unaware of our continually arising thoughts, which are often subtle, we end up identifying with them. This identification or attachment is largely responsible for the widely held belief, "I'm thinking," and again, the belief in a central, permanent Self. One or more supposedly supreme thoughts criticize, judge, or tell the other thoughts to go away.

But I wish these thoughts would go away is clearly just another thought, given authority by attachment and identification. It's a supreme or lead thought that thinks it is in charge. Funny, right? It, too, is simply another thought – no me, no you, just what it is. No more, no less.

This lead thought or thoughts, and our belief in a Self results in a subtle thought that thinks it is the mindful observer. This also recreates the thought hierarchy, a divided mind, and many life conflicts. I'm mindful and I'm a good or bad meditator also arises and is believed as part of the supposed Self. This causes tremendous suffering in daily life and hinders our practice at all levels until it is seen and understood clearly.

So, what to do? Keep it simple. Have a soft resolve to catch or be mindful of the very beginnings of thought when you meditate or are quiet, as often as you can. Don't believe me; see for yourself: The thinker is the thought, or the thought is the thinker, however you want to say it. Thought arises, and we quickly identify with it because it is not seen clearly or early enough. This results in the thought and belief that someone is thinking! Thoughts come and go by their own nature, much like the breath. Can we see this, moment to moment?

Let's take a look and see directly for ourselves if this is true. Don't overthink it, just see it. Deep wisdom will change your life, and you will smile!

Meditation Exercise
The Thinking Game

Settle in, and get comfy. Close your eyes and relax – smile – the dearest friends, teachers of transformation, and guardians of the heart will be seen and known through your awareness of the present. They are ready to guide, teach and protect you.

In the Thinking Game, our only job is to be an aware gatekeeper of the mind and see the first instant of arising thought.

*Pause as you wish during this meditation exercise.

Rest in the body, as if it's a chair at the movies, including the movies of the mind. Let the body relax and act as a ground – simply being aware.

Thoughts and images have already started because the movie waits for no one. Can you see that it's not generated by someone or "you," that it happens largely by itself? Please hear me; this understanding will save you a lot of suffering!

During this exercise, it's OK if you want to use a mental note as an aid. Each time a thought arises, it's enough to simply label it thinking, thinking. But be fully aware of that, also.

Try to catch (without tension) the first syllable of thought or inkling of an image as it arises. No attachment to content. Relax, no stress. Let go at first glance. Observe without judging, but if there is judgment, see that at its first bloom.

See and let go, see and let go – your only job at this movie show! Perhaps you will see that thoughts don't stay long if they are not fed.

See how they come uninvited. Arrive from stillness, stay, leave back to stillness.

See how they come and go of themselves and stay or leave on their own terms and conditions.

When we are bothered by them, we breathe life into the story. We do the same if we like them. But if they are seen as what they are – simply another cloud rolling through the big sky of the mind – then the question of what to do with thought is quietly answered. No pushing, no pulling, just being aware.

See if the mind can rest in natural awareness before thought. If it can, then the true definition of "just being" is seen, and the issue of thought and the Self begins to transform naturally. You can't do it, but it can be done. If these statements make sense, great. If not, don't worry; they will be clear to you at some point as you continue to walk the path with a smile.

Remember, welcome and accept all the visitors as friends, including thought, without trying to control them. Rest in loving awareness, it is your friend for life.

A student once said to Ajahn Chah, "I still have many thoughts, and my mind wanders a lot, even though I'm trying to be mindful."

The great Thai forest master replied, "Don't worry about this. Just try to keep your mind in the present. Whatever arises in the mind, just watch it, and let go of it. Don't even wish to be rid of thoughts."

Encouraging the student to drop notions of self and other and focus, in a simple way, on "just what there is" in the present moment, Ajahn Chah went on to say: "Wherever you are, know yourself by being natural and watching. If doubts arise, watch them come and go ... Everything is changing. Whatever you pass, don't cling to it ... All things will come and go of themselves."

This is a universal law – don't fight it; you will suffer much less.

Chapter 24

The Inherent Truth of Inclusivity

Welcome and smile – this is your precious human life.

If you stay on the path of mindfulness, you will find each friend, teacher, and guardian in your own way and your own time. Be assured, with deep faith and confidence, they will appear!

As you continue on this journey, one particular truth that will emerge is the importance and beneficial alignment of having a deep sense of inclusivity for all beings in your heart – a profound recognition of our interconnectedness and interdependence with all of life.

In a world full of so much discord and disconnection, our spiritual work in this area has never been more important. Because whatever you think of yourself, you do matter, and others matter too! You will always matter to the community of spiritual friends.

Connection is what often helps us deal with the dark corners and dangerous neighborhoods of the mind. Sangha, friends and family – people who care about each other – make a huge difference in our spiritual life and life in general.

As we divide, we forget about the art and benefit of communication with skillful, wise speech, particularly when it comes to getting along with "difficult people." As studies and maybe our own lives have shown, things like social media and the internet, which promised to bring us together, have, in many instances, had the opposite effect.

Research shows that today, both young and old are more removed from face-to-face interaction. This near-universal reliance on texting, social media, email, etc., may result in isolation, lower self-esteem, higher anxiety levels, anger, and depression. Often people are meaner, ruder, and more aggressive online than they would ever dream of being in person. Have you noticed?

Perfectionistic self-presentation (100 selfie attempts for that one perfect shot that we post) and social isolation move us away from the truth that we are all deeply interconnected and need inclusion and fellowship. See if this is true: Are we inherently social whether we like it or not? The Buddha certainly recognized the benefits of interdependence and interconnection by insisting his monks go into the local village for alms rounds (food freely given by villagers), with the monks then reciprocating that support by teaching and assisting the village with spiritual guidance and other matters.

A sense of inclusiveness comes as we walk the path of awakening and see clearly that we are far more alike than different. We all want freedom from suffering. We all have inherent goodness toward compassion and deep affection for ourselves and others, regardless of where they or we sit.

I mentioned a while ago to some meditation friends that I was blessed with lots of friends on both sides of the political spectrum. Someone said, "I have no Republican friends," and later, another said, "I have no Democrat friends." What are we doing?

If we are no more than our thoughts, moods, and opinions, we're all in deep trouble. Did Mother Teresa care who the poor and sick voted for, or was she motivated by compassion and love so much deeper than the whims of constantly changing thoughts, moods, and opinions?

Can we see if this is true – that our path must be aligned in this way for goodness, affection, and insight to arise, that there can't be "us and them," or our heart is still divided?

I was robbed by a pickpocket on a trip to Jerusalem some time ago. After the initial shock subsided, my heart quickly aligned to the serenity and acceptance of what couldn't be changed. By not taking it personally, no animus arose. The universe clearly said, "The pickpocket needed your phone more than you did, so let it go!" Loving kindness also arose. It was an inconvenience for a time. I wished he hadn't done it, but the whole episode became just a footnote of the trip.

Our web of interdependence and interconnection is vast. Our recognition of this shouldn't just be intellectual – appreciation and a natural affection will arise from seeing clearly and developing a heart that includes all beings. Our lifelong question also arises: Does our heart have enough room and love to include this, too? For "them," too?

Ultimately, empathy, affection, and compassion for all sentient beings will drive your spiritual path. I learned early on that deep suffering is the same in all – content is different, but the process is the same.

Generosity, morality, forgiveness, natural kindness, and many other awakened values move in lockstep with a deeply felt recognition of inclusivity.

A deep understanding of your own inclusivity contains affection and compassion for all beings, including yourself, with the difficult ones turning into dear ones. We then naturally do our work for the good and happiness of all beings as if they were our own – as they ultimately truly are.

A Heart Which Includes all Beings: Inclusivity, Mindfulness and Natural Loving Kindness Exercise

Let's settle into the body with a sense of warmth and affection for all sentient beings. Smile, we all have this precious human life full of friends, teachers, and guardians to walk with us, hand in hand.

*Pause during the exercise where and when, as you see fit.

Let the mind rest in loving awareness that simply sees without wanting to change anything – just observing. Feel the affection and sense of care that may arise.

Feel the natural alignment of mind toward open-heartedness – does our heart have enough room and love for whatever arises?

Can we agree no one wants to suffer – just like us – and all want to love and be loved – just like us?

Reflect on what it took to be here. Of all the family, friends, and kind people who helped you arrive wherever you are. Also, reflect on all of the stuff of your life, your house or apartment, food, clothes, healthy body and mind, and the things you need to survive and thrive.

A sense of gratitude naturally arises in the heart with just a glance at what went "right" for us to be here. It's an infinite web of interconnectedness with our needs that have been nurtured and touched by some we will know and huge numbers we will never know.

Imagine the countless interdependent and interconnected sentient beings. Relax in the comfort that you are deeply cared about. You do matter and are appreciated. Know this.

Can the heart be tender and feel affection for all? An endearment for others because, as Mother Teresa says, "We do belong to each other." When we forget this, we forget our deepest purpose in life.

Let your heart open to the warmth and affection for all, with a deep bow of appreciation! As inclusivity arrives, you will see the world with a fresh new kindness as a gift for all you meet, along with your smile.

"All of spiritual practice is a matter of relationship: to ourselves, to others, to life's situations. We can relate with a spirit of wisdom, compassion, and flexibility, or we can meet life with fear, aggression, and delusion. Whether we like it or not, we are always in relationship, always interconnected."

"Expanding our spiritual practice is actually a process of expanding our heart, of widening our circle of insight and compassion to gradually include the whole of our life. Being on earth here in human bodies, this year, this night, is our spiritual practice."

– Jack Kornfield

Lastly, in a world full of so much disconnection, our spiritual work has never been more important. Why do we do this work? Because we understand our interconnectedness and that, for us to survive, our practice must be dedicated to the happiness and freedom of all living creatures.

Chapter 25

Learning to Dance With the Difficult With Gratitude and Appreciation

It warms my heart and brings a smile to my face knowing we're still together.

I want to talk about gratitude with appreciation. As you know, these continue to be difficult and trying times, so we need skillful antidotes to help us adapt and cope. Both gratitude and appreciation, like mindfulness, allow you to bring light into darkness, helping to provide a balanced, skillful perspective when things are difficult or unsettled.

I have a deep sense of gratitude and appreciation for so many things, especially all the tremendously hard work people have done over these difficult years to keep each other, and sanghas as a whole, connected and together.

But it's not just about feeling gratitude, warmth, and affection. It's about benefiting others by taking action.

Gratitude is one of the many important shades of joy and is very similar to the Brahma-vihara of sympathetic joy for the happiness of others. It is also the feeling that moves, in my mind, to an appreciation for all the lessons of life and the sentient beings in it – especially the "difficult" ones.

Remember, whatever adversity knocks on your door in life, you can, with time and practice, develop your immediate

Mona Lisa smile. It arises and says, 'Welcome, come in; you are accepted and appreciated as my teacher.' In Buddhism, this gladdening of the mind arises as the many energies we call joy.

At first, this smile may feel not so convincing, but with the willingness to keep answering life's door, you will see for yourself that you actually mean the "welcome" and that the smile naturally arises. It is a remarkable transformation. For example, as I've aged, it has become very easy to see what I've lost – family, friends, and physical changes that can move you to dark "neighborhoods" of the mind.

I loved visiting my grandfather, particularly as he and I grew older. He often told me the same stories with some slight variations, but I fully enjoyed them no matter what, as I felt a deep bond and fellowship with him. I also felt his loneliness and sense of isolation (common, especially for the elderly) even though he was blessed with many grandchildren and others. One day, he told me I was the only one who came to visit (hopefully, that was not true). "The only time I leave my apartment is for another funeral," he said.

I always left my grandfather with a heartfelt smile and my love; he always reciprocated with light in his eyes! But it was sad that he so easily moved into the darker corners and neighborhoods of the mind. At the time, I didn't know some of the natural antidotes or how to dance with the difficult. I wish I had known then what I know now: Gratitude with appreciation allows you to smile more often and break free of the darkness or the difficulties of older age. It gives you a larger, more skillful perspective and wisdom. You appreciate all the things you still have and can still do.

I wake up many mornings with a deep sense of gratitude filled with soft insight joy, that moves into thankfulness and appreciation for many things, but especially for this precious human life, with its highs and lows, difficulties, and beautiful vistas. It is a life full of opportunities for growth, freedom, and the joy of serving others. Discovering and acting on these truths can help save your life, as it did mine.

Especially these days, I wake up with a vast sense of gratitude for all of you, the spiritual friends that continue to support communities of goodness and each other with your smiles and gracious, generous hearts. I deeply appreciate how you continue to do this even after being challenged by the pandemic, illness, and many worries.

You show up each day, wherever you are, with the purity of intention and persistence to do the work necessary to walk the path through the easy or the difficult times. I also feel an insight joy for those who see the importance of sitting quietly and seeing things as they truly are, not necessarily how they want them to be.

It is a larger perspective of gratitude with deep affection and wisdom that knows we show up on this journey for each other and all sentient beings because it is the only wise, skillful thing to do in response to this difficult world! To open our heart and mind even to the difficult, knowing our purity of heart will save us, just as division often attempts to divide and destroy us.

Lastly, there is a gratitude towards the world communities of goodness that especially now needs to see our deep inherent interconnection, from Buddha nature for Buddhists and by grace as we are all children of God for Christians. Also, gratitude for the importance of compassionate action from all of us working together for the benefit of billions of people we will likely never know or ever meet!

Once your heart and mind have been touched by this deep gratitude with appreciation, even for a moment, you may have noticed the smile I've talked about. It's the beginning of truth shining through as our heart begins to heal, knowing our life's purpose of affection and compassion for all.

Gratitude Exercise

Let's do a simple meditation reflection to help us see this gratitude with appreciation.

*Pause during the exercise where and when, as you see fit.

Relax – be aware and connect with your body. Embody the body with affectionate awareness.

Smile – you have been given a precious human life; reflect on those friends who care for and love you. In that care and love is a sense of safety. Feel the natural gratitude that warms your heart.

Reflect on the gift of hearing and a brain to process that allows each of us the ability to learn and grow.

Let's move back in time a little and realize that even in a difficult life, it is skillful to reflect on the ones that cared for you and kept you safe until you could make your own way. The Buddha said, "If you carried your parents on your shoulders for your adult life, you could not repay the debt you owe them."

Reflect on the gift of a body that still works, perhaps just not as well as it once did, but smile in appreciation for the opportunities we still have.

Smile at the difficulties you've come through and all of those who have been with you through all the storms and those with whom you have enjoyed the vistas and beautiful sunsets.

Reflect on the many things – food, water, clothes, a roof over your head, and the other "stuff" of life, which all help to sustain and protect you.

Reflect on the many people you can imagine responsible for the food, roads, our health, and protection. For the pets, and the people that make you smile and the compassion you have for the ones that don't.

Finally, reflect on the millions and millions you don't know, but are still deeply interconnected with. Feel the gratitude leading to (the action of) appreciation because we must get along and work together, knowing we belong to each other. Smile, we do belong here!

Chapter 26

SMILE – An Acronym for Living in an Unsettled World With Goodness, Discovery, and Truth
A Guided Exercise – Transforming Anger Moving From SMILE to SMILES

It warms my heart and brings a smile to my face to know, as you finish this book, we are still together as we walk this path of goodness, discovery, and truth. I wrote this book for those who had, have, or will have a darkness they may not know how to survive or move past toward the light of goodness. There is a way through. It begins with a flicker of light, the light of mindfulness with goodness and all the gifts, friends, teachers, and guardians that come along the way. This includes the real possibility of an extraordinary, precious life guided by wisdom and compassion, with affection for all beings.

In this chapter, the focus is on bringing meditation into action, through a guided exercise using our expanded version of SMILE – SMILES. This acronym will help you remember many of our most important friends, teachers, and guardians for a more skillful, balanced, and joyful life.

Settle in, and relax into the body. Relaxation is extremely important as it contains qualities of trust, an attitude of come what may, and welcoming the present moment (the only true moment) for the teacher and the teachings each moment contains. Relaxation also starts to release, loosen, and diminish the fabric or density of our deeply conditioned belief in a permanent solid "self" or "ego," which covers up the inherently pure nature of the heart.

Relaxation is also important since tension always has an element of constriction, holding and tightening the mind, body, or both. Insight arises most easily when both are relaxed and generally, insight or awakening only happens when the mind opens to the present moment, not when it constricts.

For our exercise with SMILES, we'll use anger as our difficult energy to explore. We all know anger, how it feels and that, although it's deeply biological, it is also almost always a conditioned reaction (2nd arrow). Something happens in life that we don't like. From our deep conditioning, we react and pick anger as our unskillful "gift" to give to ourselves or another.

With mindfulness (awareness) present, we have a chance to respond skillfully without anger. There is a split-second, silent reflection before we react. This sacred pause allows us choices to respond skillfully, with wisdom and clarity, instead of causing harm by reacting from old conditioning.

However, anger can be a deep, dangerous, reactive mind state. We need to bring awareness as early as possible to respond safely to ourselves and others. Let's find a small, manageable annoyance or anger of yours to practice with. It could be a slightly annoying person, thing, situation or whatever you can bring up safely. You know yourself and what is manageable for you; don't pick a person or situation that you could find to be overwhelming. After your practice deepens, perhaps the "unmanageable" can become manageable and addressed later.

Relax once again and notice the energy of anger in the body, the ebb and flow of sensations that often appear solid but never really are. Recognize, accept, and feel these sensations in the ever-present body. Notice the feeling tone of anger, the heat, tension, and tightness. Try not to add dialogue, and be sure to turn down the volume of your commentary. It almost always feeds anger and increases its grip. Remember, the body is the main ground in meditation. Use it often, and become embodied in the body.

Notice how anger manifests in the body and colors the mind. The body is not the primary verbal storyteller; the mind's content seduces with thoughts and mental and physical reactions. Don't buy the story or the dialogue; it feeds more anger. Smile – it's OK! Just let it be, since it's there. Give most of your attention to the bodily sensations of anger. Let's move to SMILES.

S   Now comes the first S in SMILES, which is to have an actual physical (Mona Lisa) smile, as our first skillful action. This will help the early surrender or welcome of anger. This does not mean giving in and giving it to another. In the first instant of our soft smile, feel the sea/see change that reduces the aggressive aspects of anger. It says, "Welcome. Come in, my friend anger. You are accepted and appreciated by me as my teacher." Feel this change of attitude and perspective that our smile with a welcome has on the mind and body.

This smile is an acceptance of what is. It begins to plant seeds of friendship and love, preparing the mind and heart for a surrender that comes from a place of strength and courage, verified faith. This is the deep, abiding confidence that comes from knowing firsthand the accuracy, goodness and truth of the teachings and the Dharma. This smile into surrender also says to anger, "You can teach me, but you can't hurt me anymore!"

Surrender is not giving in or identifying with what is in this moment, but rather allowing or accepting the uniqueness of the now and the friends, teachers, and guardians that begin to arrive. (Take a quiet moment to reflect on this.)

M   This smile and attitude/perspective change allows us to naturally come into the M in SMILE, which is to settle into the present moment, the only moment you have, with affectionate mindfulness. Mindfulness is the great protector of you and others. It brings additional, wholesome factors of mind, including joy, investigation, love, and equanimity, to mention a few. This makes it very difficult for anger to refuel or grow.

Mindfulness is perhaps our most important dearest friend, teacher of transformation, and guardian of the heart. Without its presence, it is impossible to see clearly or penetrate delusion and confusion, which is necessary for wisdom and insight to arise. Allow mindfulness to arise as early as you can before any painful "aspect" of anger is given to another. See anger with acceptance because it's there – and can be a very useful teacher. Relax; this may also be the beginning of loosening the fabric of delusion and confusion. See for yourself!

I The I in SMILE is for Investigation, which arises naturally as one of mindfulness's first and most important friends. A curiosity or probing quality of mind, investigation is one of the primary wisdom factors of mindfulness. Smile as wisdom will begin to teach you now. Investigate as you become aware of the interplay of mind-objects and the reactions in the body to anger. See how anger can burn you first and can poison and harden your heart with hatred if not skillfully dealt with (reflect). Investigation also brings interest, increasing natural focus by unifying the energies of the mind. It's very similar to what happens when you hear a good story. It's a natural focus or effortless concentration for discovery and insight.

Smile; you can make friends with anger and come to even deeper wisdom. We now have the SMI of SMILE, which is smile with surrender (acceptance), mindfulness and investigation.

L Investigation brings wisdom, which arrives with one of our first, simplest, and most profound teachings: Letting go, the L of SMILE. As you mindfully settle into this moment, fully allowing and accepting whatever arises, you may find love in your heart again as you move to a deep sense of letting be. Love begins to arise as you realize anger loses its power of control by not being fed through dialogue and reaction. This allows the natural affection of the heart's recognition that "Anger cannot harm me or others anymore." With love, you will smile naturally and easily.

Remember, "letting go" is often a continuum from letting go a little (you suffer a lot) to letting go a lot (you suffer a little) until you ultimately arrive at letting be. Letting be in its truest form is complete "hands off," as the mind rests in selfless awareness with no will to change anything. No push, no pull, just what there is, as complete acceptance of the present moment as it is complete.

Also, the natural state of our heart is affection or love, but it can be easily covered over by anger or animus. Can you let go or let be so completely that all trace of suffering from anger is transformed into the joy or love of release? As you have hopefully now discovered for yourself, moving from letting go to deep letting be contains the natural seeds of love and the joy of acceptance. As our teacher, we joyfully embrace each moment, and all it contains. Reflect on this.

With the arrival of letting be until you love, you are also now ready for our letter E of SMILE.

E   Letting be until you love naturally leads to Equanimity, the E in SMILE, which also allows for engagement. As the mind releases a little or completely any object of mind, equanimity arises, with its strength or completeness determined by the degree of letting go, and creates a balance where you and others are now safe. Equanimity from insight is one of the most stable, durable, and balanced friends of mindfulness and all meditation practices.

S   You are Safe because the energy of anger has transmuted into a sense of love (affection) and balance in your heart. This is our final S, making SMILES. You now are a refuge for all beings, fully prepared for skillful engagement. You have finally arrived at SMILES, so bring your smiles to the world community. You now have the ability to give a beautiful gift to everyone you meet: safe, skillful engagement with a smile.

> *"At the moment of waking up, before getting out of bed,*
> *get in touch with your breath,*
> *feel the various sensations in your body,*
> *note any thoughts and feeling that may be present,*
> *let mindfulness touch this moment,*
> *Can you feel your breath?*
> *Can you perceive the dawning of each in breath?*
> *Can you enjoy the feeling of the breath freely*
> *entering your body in this moment?*
> *'Breathe in, I smile, breathe out, I calm my body,*
> *dwelling in the present moment, it is a wonderful moment.'"*
>
> *– Thich Nhat Hanh*

Finally, know you are always loved and appreciated as a fellow traveler on life's most important journey of goodness, discovery, and truth!

May the truth guide you, may the truth protect you, and may the truth surround you and all beings with love and kindness guided by wisdom and compassion each and every day for the rest of your life!

May it be so, and know you are a marvel to the world!

Loving Kindness Through Engaged Purity of Heart Smile – the Special Sauce of Heart and Wisdom Practices

As spiritual friends, we know many are in need of our kind, reassuring presence. A presence that includes the long arms of mindfulness, wisdom, and compassion to reach, hold and care for all those who have suffering and pain in all forms.

For those who live without daily bread, may we help bring relief from hunger through our actions and generosity. The Buddha said, "If you knew what I know about generosity, you wouldn't let a single meal pass without offering some to someone."

For those who live with fear and heartache, may we help them come to peace, joy, and real happiness through our spiritual courage and action.

For those who live with physical or mental pain, may we help all beings find peace, equanimity, and the health and healing from the loving hands they need.

For those who live without the love and warmth of family and friends, may we actually seek them out and bring companionship and kind, gentle, kindred spirits along the way.

For those who live with injustice and prejudice, may we be the voices that are heard and help bring justice with clear eyes and a balanced, loving heart.

And for all beings who live in exile from the truth, may we as sangha help them find the strength and sincerity to take that next step, no matter how difficult or small, in the direction of purity of heart and transformation, a work we always do for all of humanity!

Be safe, stay healthy, and know you are loved and appreciated!

About The Author

Mark W. Gebert is a guiding teacher and cofounder of Roswell Insight Meditation Community in Georgia. He began his meditation practice almost 50 years ago with his lifelong teacher Joseph Goldstein. He has also studied for decades with, and been a friend of, guiding senior insight teachers Rodney Smith and Narayan Helen Liebenson. Mark's teaching comes from what he calls "the school of keep it simple," with an emphasis on the essentials for a skillful, wise, affectionate life. His journey tells the story of how mindfulness can provide opportunities for transformation, which he calls the Marvels of Mindfulness, in all aspects of one's life. He has completed three

3-month retreats as well as dozens of others and has studied in both Tibetan and Zen traditions. He is a retired doctoral-level psychologist and 25-year crisis intervention coordinator/team leader, as well as an ordained Christian deacon. Mark has been married to the love of his life for over 40 years. They have two children and two grandchildren and have lived on Marvel Ridge in the foothills of the Appalachians for more than 35 years.

Index

2nd arrow,108,139,142,143, 190, 201
Anapanasati Sutta,88
anicca,14,127,169
awareness,x,xiii,3,4,6,23,24,26, 52,55,56,57,59,71,72,84,86,87, 88,90,91,94,95,100,102,103,105 ,110,114,135,139,140,148,149, 158,162,167,169,170,171,173, 174,180,187,190,194
beginner's mind,57,74,99
Big Sky Mind,90
Bodhisattva,34,113
Brahama-viharas,xiv,60,101, 109,152,153,155,
Buddha,vi,vii,x,9,24,37,38,39, 68,72,74,82,84,85,102,117,120, 122,127,147,177,186,187, 197
choiceless awareness,xiii, 56,85,86,88,89,90,91
compassion,xiii,5,8,27,29,31,34, 38,40,41,43,44,46,49,52,59,60,6 1,62,64,76,77,97,99,102,107,10 8,111,112,113,114,115,122,123, 124,130,131,134,141,149,150, 152,154,155,156,157,158,159, 160,165,177,178,179,181,186, 188,189,196,197
concentration,xii,xiii,22,25,60, 68,72,73,75,79,82,83,84,85,86, 87,88,92,94,138,193
dark night of the soul,21
dedicated practice,32,34,59,113
delusion,2,6,15,17,18,24,36,46, 47,60,69,70,71,74,84,124,125, 127,129,131,132,138,140,158, 159,181,192,193
Dharma,vii,23,56,59,62,72,192,
dukkha,14, 127
Ehipassiko,vii,xi,29,36,37,38,39

Eight Worldly Winds,100
emptiness,113, 169
energy,xii,10,12,21,25,68,69,70, 72,75,77,78,79,80,81,83.85,92, 104,133,134,136,137,138,143, 190,195
equanimity,ix,xiii,7,9,10,12,21, 22,25,26,32,53,60,68,73,80,94, 98,100,101,102,104,108,138, 143,145,152,153,154,156,157, 160,192,194,195,197
exclusive concentration, 72,83,84,85,87,88,92,94
external locus of control, 146,147,148,150
factors of mind, 4,14,27,70,71,192,193
far enemies, xiv,153,154,157,158,159,160,
Four Perfections or Purities of the Heart,152
generosity,xiii,27,29,76,108,117 118,120,122,123,140,141,179, 197
Generosity,117
Gladdening The Mind, xiii,92
gratitude,v,xiii,xv,2,27,29,47,51 93,96,108,140,180,183,184,185, 186,187,188
greed,xiv,2,30,46,47,69,70,79, 84,100,117,118,123,124,125,12 6,127,131,132,133,141,153,158, 159
hatred,25,46,69,84,126,139,153, 158,159,193
hindrances,xiv,32,68,69,70,85, 132,136,142
Hindrances, 13
hungry ghosts, 84

inclusive concentration 85,86,87,88
inclusivity,xv,27,109,120,176, 179,180,181
insight,v,vii,vii,x,5,6,9,13,19,20, 24,25,38,51,55,60,66,68, 71,73,75,78,79,80,83,87,94,95, 100,103,111,112,132,140,152, 157,164,178,181,185,190,193, 195,199
internal locus of control, 146,148,150
investigation,v,ix,xi,xii,7,12,24, 25,27,30,32,33,34,37,38,68,71, 72,74,75,76,78,85,92,94,103,10 4,144,166,192,193
Jhana,83,85
karma,120,146
karmic,77,154
karuna,152
kundalini,80,81
letting be,7,12, 15,43,47,73,94,100,105,135,145 193,194,
letting go, ix,7,12,15,42,43,47,50,73,86,88, 94,100,132,135,138,145,153, 164,193,194
loving kindness, 27,46,59,60,61,76,83,95,101,10 7,111,112,114,152,153,155
LovingKindness, 14,15,60,131,152,178,180,197
mantra,118
mantras,83
metta,60,61,152
Middle Way,38,133
mindfulness (*sati*), 2
morality,xiii,27,108,117,120, 121,122,179
mudita,93,152,153
near enemies,xiv,109,152,155, 159,160

papancha,78,137
precepts,21,120
reconciliation,42,44
redemption,42,44
right view,4
sacred pause,26,101,129,190
samvega,5, 7
Sangha,x,xii,5,7,13,36,37,51,52 58,61,62,143,149,176,183, 198,
Seven Factors of Enlightenment,68
skillful means, 5,10,38,52,108,132,135,142
Skillful Means,59,151,180,183
spiritual urgency,ix, xii,13,17
sympathetic joy,93,152,154,183
teasing apart,158
tranquility,xiii,21,25,68,72,73, 83,92,93,94,95,96,97,104,138
transformation,v,ix,xi,xiii,1,2,4, 6,7,8,13,23,25,27,29,34,42,44, 49,52,66,68,70,75,78,84,87,102, 106,111,127,128,131,149,160, 161,169,173,184,192,198,199
truth,ii,vi,vii,xi,xv,2,3,4,8,13,18, 27,28,31,34,36,37,38,41,49,51, 52,56,59,64,67,74,82,98,103, 105,107,109,121,123,148,149, 154,160,176,177,185,186,189, 192,196,198
unfabricated awareness,90
universal law,127,129,158, 175
universal laws,169,170
upekkha,101,152,153
vipassana,94
worldcommunity,26,125,143, 145,195

Made in the USA
Middletown, DE
15 March 2024

51593197R00121